THE POWER OF DESIRE

Also by Wes Berry

Motivational Leadership & Business Series

Big Things Have Small Beginnings: The Motivation and Mindset that Build a $750-Million Business (Book 1)

Success Factors: Million-Dollar Concepts that Work for Everyone (Book 2)

The Power of Desire: Your Toolbox for Success (Book 3)

Business Quick Reads Series

The Positive Side of Golf: Motivation

Ice Cream Therapy: Mindset

Icons of Success: Leadership

The Ritz Experience: Growth and Scalability

Ty Cobb, Babe Ruth, and So On: Teamwork

The Right Stuff: Integrity

The Two Steves: Core Competencies

FUD Moneyball: Change

Get on Board: Inclusion

Stress Is My Superpower

Outcome Based Sales

Effective Communication

Master the Metaverse: Multi-Million Dollar Investment Opportunities

Praise for
Big Things Have Small Beginnings
By Wes Berry

Wall Street Journal Bestseller

USA TODAY Bestseller

Barnes & Noble's Top 5 Best Sellers of All Books Worldwide

Amazon #1 Best Selling Author, #1 Hot New Release, and International Best Seller

Business Insider, Books to Help You Build Wealth and Get More Done

New York Book Festival, Winner Best Business Book

"Wes, I love your new book…I love everything about it! Keep up the great work!"

Kevin O'Leary, star of Shark Tank

"Big Things Have Small Beginnings is the truest thing I've heard! I'm all about it!"

Bethenny Frankel, CEO of Skinnygirl

"I'm looking at this line from Wes Berry's book, which I really loved. 'The fear of failure has prevented more success than actual failure has.' Go out there, take the risk. It's worth it."

Jason Feifer, Editor-in-Chief of Entrepreneur magazine

"Congratulations on winning first place in the Southern California Book Festival for 'Big Things have Small Beginnings.' Congratulations, Wes! Keep changing lives!"

Daymond John, CEO of FUBU

"A foundation of ideas with which to succeed in virtually every aspect of life."

John J. Kelly, Detroit Free Press

"Wise and warm counsel from a man who makes small beginnings blossom into success."

Grady Harp, Amazon Hall of Fame Top 50 Reviewer

"An enlightening and extremely informative book!"

Susan Keefe, Midwest Book Review

"If you are in business, or want to be, read this book."

Mike Ball, Erma Bombeck award-winning columnist

"This book will propel you to the top of your business game!"

Pamela Gossiaux, International Bestselling Author

WALL STREET JOURNAL
bestselling author

THE POWER OF DESIRE

YOUR TOOLBOX FOR SUCCESS

Includes a 21-Day Challenge

WES BERRY

Motivational Leadership & Business Series Volume 3

Copyright © 2024 by Green Dragon Services LLC

All rights reserved.

This book or any portion thereof may not be reproduced or used in any manner whatsoever without the express written permission of the publisher except for the use of brief quotations in a book review.

ISBN: 979-8-9905998-1-9 (paperback)

ISBN: 979-8-9905998-2-6 (hardcover)

ISBN 979-8-9905998-3-3 (ebook)

Visit the author's website at
WesBerryGroup.com
for more information.

Published in the United States of America.

DEDICATION

To my dear wife and sons,

I dedicate this book to that one individual who has always been by my side, supporting me through thick and thin. You are my rock, my guiding light, and the reason why I strive to be a better person every day. Yes, Winston, you are my best friend, a real bulldog, and the unsung hero behind this book. Your snorts and snores have been the soundtrack to my writing process, and your endless supply of drool has provided much-needed inspiration during the ruff times. Sometimes you growl; however, your bark is always worse than your bite.

Oh, and to my wife and kids - you guys are cool too. Thanks for putting up with my eccentricities and always being loving and thoughtful about applauding when Winston rolls over.

Table of Contents

Part 1: Define Your Desire

Chapter 1. Why Desired Outcomes Matter:
Unleashing the Power of Vision……………….....21

Chapter 2. The Anatomy of a Desired Outcome:
Clarity, Specificity, and Meaning……………….29

Chapter 3. The Art of Goal-Setting:
SMART Criteria and Beyond…………………....37

Chapter 4. The Science of Motivation:
Intrinsic vs. Extrinsic Drivers…………………...43

Chapter 5. The Role of Values, Purpose, and Identity
in Desired Outcomes…………………………….49

Chapter 6. The Power Trio: Visualization,
Affirmation, and Meditation………………..……55

Chapter 7. The Cognitive Skills, Abilities, and
Intuitive Thinking that Drive Success……………63

Chapter 8. Positive Thinking: Unlocking Your Path
to Success and Happiness…………………….....75

Part 2: Pursue Your Desire

Chapter 9. Mapping Your Terrain: PESTLE Analysis
and Environmental Scanning…………………….85

Chapter 10. Developing Your Strategy:
SWOT Matrix……………………….…….93

Chapter 11. Developing Your Strategy:
Porter's Five Forces……………………..…103

Chapter 12. Creating Your Action Plan:
To-Do Lists, and Milestones………..………111

Chapter 13. Building Your Support Network: Mentors,
Allies, and Accountability Partners…………121

Chapter 14. Managing Your Resources: Time,
Money, and Energy…………………….……129

Chapter 15. Cultivating Your Skills and Knowledge:
Learning Plans and Self-Development….…..137

Part 3: Attain Your Desire
Chapter 16. Assessing Your Progress: Key Performance Indicators and Metrics...........147
Chapter 17. Overcoming Obstacles: Procrastination, Perfectionism, and Self-Sabotage..............155
Chapter 18. Facing Your Fears: Failure, Rejection, and Criticism..........................165
Chapter 19. Learning from Feedback: Feedback Loops, Surveys, and Reviews..................179
Chapter 20. Staying on Track: Habit Formation, Routines, and Rituals............................189
Chapter 21. Sustaining Your Momentum: Continuous Improvement and Growth Mindset............195
Chapter 22. Celebrating Your Achievements: Milestone Parties, Gratitude Journals, and Rewards..201
Chapter 23. Making Your Desired Outcome a Legacy: Giving Back, Paying Forward, and Contributing to Society..........................208

21-Day Challenge..216
About the Author..282

INTRODUCTION

Are you ready to define, pursue, and attain your desired outcomes?

Have you ever heard the saying, "If you don't know where you're going, any road will get you there"? It's a humorous way of highlighting the importance of setting clear goals. When we have a clear idea of what we want to achieve, we are more likely to take action and make progress towards our desired outcome. But setting goals is not always easy—it requires self-reflection, careful planning, and a willingness to take risks.

That's where desire comes in— it is a powerful motivator that can fuel our actions and drive us towards our goals. When we have a powerful desire for something, we are more likely to put in the effort and make sacrifices to achieve it. But desire alone is not enough—we also need the right tools and guidance to help us define, pursue, and attain our desired outcomes.

This is where studying this book, *The Power of Desire* comes in—it is a comprehensive guide to achieving success and fulfillment by harnessing the power of our desires. The book offers a flexible framework that can be tailored to our unique goals and circumstances. It is not a one-size-fits-all solution, but rather a collection of principles, practices, and examples that can inspire and guide us on our journey towards our desired outcome.

One of the key aspects of achieving our desired outcomes is motivation. Motivation is a critical factor in achieving success. Let's compare motivation to the skills and tools of a carpenter: even if we have all the skills and tools we need to achieve our desired outcome, (our training as a carpenter, our saws, hammers, etc.) we still need desire to get the job done. Right? In this book, I offer you the support and inspiration to help you stay motivated, along with several key recipes to evaluate and thereby engage the skills, tools, and motivation necessary to track towards your desired results.

This book is targeted towards anyone who wants to improve their life, whether you are a student, professional, entrepreneur, parent, or just someone looking to clarify your purpose, align your values, and maximize your potential. The potential outcomes that can be achieved through the book are varied; some people may want wealth and fame, while others may want happiness and love, or knowledge and creativity. This book can help readers clarify their vision and develop a plan to achieve their desired outcome.

The book is organized into four parts, each containing several chapters that delve into specific topics and provide practical tools and tips for implementation. The first 21 chapters of the book offer a 21-Day Challenge section that matches up with the information presented in the chapters, empowering readers to attain their desires. Completing the challenge will give you the tools you need for success, but you still need to stay motivated on your journey towards your desired outcome.

The journey towards our desired outcome can be tough and unpredictable, but it can also be incredibly fulfilling and transformative. The book acknowledges the challenges and unpredictability of the journey and positions itself as a companion and source of support to help you keep moving forward. As you, the reader, work towards your desired outcome, you may even discover new passions and purposes that you never knew you had. The journey is just as important as the destination, and this book is here to help readers make the most of every moment.

The Power of Desire encourages readers to define, pursue, and attain their desired outcomes. It is a starting point for the journey towards fulfillment and transformation, providing readers with the tools and guidance they need to achieve success. The book emphasizes the importance of making the most of every moment on the journey towards our desired outcomes and encourages readers to stay motivated and committed to their goals. Whether readers are looking to achieve wealth, happiness, love, knowledge, creativity, or something else entirely, *The Power of Desire* can help them get there.

So, are you ready to define, pursue, and attain your desired outcomes? Let's get started!

Reading The Power of Desire *is your starting point for a journey towards fulfillment and transformation, providing you with the tools and guidance you need to achieve success!*

PART 1

Define Your Desire

"The will to win, the desire to succeed, the urge to reach your full potential… these are the keys that will unlock the door to personal excellence."

Confucius

You need to visualize success to obtain it!

Chapter 1

Why Desired Outcomes Matter: Unleashing the Power of Vision

Have you ever found yourself scratching your head, pondering the meaning of your existence? Do you feel like you're running in circles, chasing your own tail? You're not alone in this bewildering journey we call life. Many folks out there are just as perplexed as you are, wondering what they're supposed to be doing with their time on this earth. But fear not, for there is a glimmer of hope amidst the chaos: a clear and compelling vision of what you want to achieve.

We're talking about a vision so specific, measurable, achievable, relevant, and time-bound that it would make even the most seasoned project manager proud. It's like having a roadmap to your dreams, guiding you with laser precision. Whether it's conquering a new language or building your own empire (cue the dramatic music), this vision gives your life purpose, direction, and that extra spark to make it happen. So go ahead, dream big and let your desired outcome be the guiding star that lights up your path!

So why should you care about having a desired outcome? There are several reasons:

1. *Clarity:* A desired outcome provides clarity about what you want to achieve, why it matters, and how you will know when you have achieved it. Let's say you're lost in a dense forest, surrounded by trees that seem to be playing a cruel game of hide-and-seek. Then suddenly you get the clarity you need to find your way. It tells you what you want to achieve (to find your way out), why it matters, (so you can get home and eat dinner) and how you'll know when you've reached that destination (you find the path marked HOME!). Clarity is like a superhero power for decision-making, planning, and execution. It helps you cut through the noise, focus your energy, and dodge those pesky distractions that come your way.

2. *Motivation:* Imagine having your very own cheerleading squad, complete with pom-poms and catchy chants. Well, guess what? A desired outcome is just that—a motivation generator that gets your engines revving. It's like having a voice inside your head saying, "You've got this, champ!" while simultaneously waving a banner that reads, "You're awesome, dude!" Intrinsic motivation, the kind that comes from within, ignites your curiosity, creativity, and the sheer thrill of taking on a challenge. Extrinsic motivation, on the other hand, comes from external rewards like recognition,

money, or status. When you've got both types of motivation fueling your drive, you'll be able to conquer obstacles and push through setbacks like a boss.

3. *Resilience:* A desired outcome fosters resilience to cope with adversity and bounce back from failure. Life is full of surprises. It's like a rollercoaster ride with unexpected twists and turns that makes your stomach do somersaults. But a desired outcome gives you resilience. It's like having a hidden stash of motivation and inspiration to tap into when the going gets tough. With a clear and compelling vision, you can rise above adversity and bounce back from failure with a vengeance. Resilience is the secret ingredient to achieving long-term success and fulfillment.

4. *Meaning:* Ah, the sweet nectar of meaning—the stuff that adds zest to our lives. A desired outcome is like a personal flavor enhancer, aligning your actions with your values, passions, and strengths. When you pursue a desired outcome that resonates with who you are and what you believe in, life takes on a whole new level of purpose, significance, and fulfillment. Meaning is the ultimate currency, far more valuable than all the gold in Fort Knox. *Impact.* When you achieve your desired outcome, you're not just winning the game of life for yourself, but you're also making a positive dent in the universe. Your desired

outcome has the potential to create value, solve problems, inspire others, and leave a legacy that transcends your personal interests. It's being the protagonist of your own story, using your skills and resources to make the world a better place.

How can you develop a clear and compelling vision of your desired outcome? Here are some practical exercises and tips:

1. *Reflect on your values, passions, and strengths:* Take a moment to ponder what truly matters to you. What makes your heart skip a beat with excitement? What are those activities that make you feel like you're in the zone, where time ceases to exist? And let's not forget about those unique talents and skills that make you shine. Grab a pen (or a keyboard) and jot down your thoughts. Look for patterns and themes that emerge, like finding the perfect rhythm in a catchy tune. These insights will serve as your compass in crafting your vision.

2. *Imagine your ideal future:* Close your eyes and let your imagination run wild. Visualize yourself in a future where you've achieved your desired outcome. What does it look like? How does it sound? And most importantly, how does it feel? Dive into the sensory

details of your vision, like a connoisseur savoring a fine wine. Imagine the benefits and rewards that come with your desired outcome, like being hailed as the world's best pancake flipper or having an office with a secret door that leads to your own personal workout space. But remember, no vision is complete without a few challenges and trade-offs. Embrace them too. Create a vivid mental image that makes your heart race with excitement.

3. *Set SMART goals:* SMART goals are specific, measurable, achievable, relevant, and time-bound. Break down your desired outcome into bite-sized goals that meet these criteria. It's like slicing your pizza into perfectly proportioned slices. By setting SMART goals, you can track your progress, celebrate milestones along the way, and adjust your goals as needed. Remember, every small step forward brings you closer to victory.

4. *Create a vision board:* Time to unleash your creative side! Make a vision board, whether it's a physical collage or a digital masterpiece. Gather images, quotes, symbols, and colors that speak to your desired outcome. Let it be a visual representation of your aspirations, like a mural painted by a master artist.

Hang it up in a place where you'll see it daily. Let your vision board serve as a constant reminder of what you're striving for and ignite that fire within you.

5. *Write a personal mission statement:* Ah, the power of words! Summarize your desired outcome, values, and purpose in a concise and impactful statement. Think of it as your own personal mantra that keeps you on track. Your mission statement should capture your unique identity and aspirations, like a tweet that goes viral for all the right reasons. Let it inspire you to live up to your full potential and be the best version of yourself.

6. *Get feedback and support:* You don't have to go it alone. Share your vision with trusted confidants who can offer valuable feedback and support. Seek advice from those who have walked the path before you or have wisdom to share. Collaborate with like-minded individuals who share your passion and drive. Surround yourself with a community that lifts you up and holds you accountable, fighting the good fight together.

Case Study: Richard Branson

Now, let's take a moment to learn from the success of a real-life legend—the one and only Richard Branson, the mastermind behind the Virgin Group. This man is the epitome of having a clear and compelling vision. With a dash of adventure and a sprinkle of audacity, Branson founded Virgin Records in his early twenties, setting out to disrupt the music industry and give artists more control over their destinies. He started in 1970 with a mail-order record business. By 1992, it was valued at $1 billion. From there, he soared to new heights, launching ventures like Virgin Atlantic Airways, Virgin Mobile, and even Virgin Galactic, aiming for the stars (quite literally).

"Having a clear sense of purpose can really lead to having a successful business," Branson said.

But here's the thing about Branson—he didn't just chase financial success. He says he didn't start Virgin Records to make money. He wanted to make a difference in people's lives.

He used his vision and influence to champion social and environmental causes, making a positive impact on the world around him. Branson's story is a testament to the power of a clear vision and staying true to your values. So, take a page from his playbook and create a life that reflects your authentic self while making a difference in the world.

Conclusion

To wrap it all up, having a clear and compelling vision of your desired outcome is like having a compass that guides you through the vast sea of possibilities. It provides you with clarity, motivation, resilience, meaning, and the ability to make a lasting impact. So, dare to dream, chase your vision with unwavering determination, and embrace the adventure that awaits. You have the power to create a life that's not only successful but also filled with laughter, joy, and a few memorable moments of hilarious triumph.

Chapter 2

The Anatomy of a Desired Outcome: Clarity, Specificity, and Meaning

Just having a desired outcome isn't going to cut it if you want to reach the promised land of success and fulfillment. You must have a crystal-clear vision of what you're after and why it's worth the sweat and tears. Lucky for you, this chapter is here to guide you through the nitty-gritty of crafting a killer desired outcome. So, buckle up and get ready to take some notes, because we're about to dive into the anatomy of what makes a truly compelling and achievable desire.

Clarity: Shining the Light on Your Destination

Clarity is the first essential element of a desired outcome. It's like the lighthouse that guides your ship through stormy seas. It's about having a clear understanding of what you want to achieve, why you want to achieve it, and how you'll know when you've reached your destination. Without clarity, you're just wandering aimlessly in a sea of possibilities.

To achieve clarity, we need to answer three crucial questions:

1. *What do you want to achieve?* Be specific and measurable. Instead of saying, "I want to be successful," say, "I want to launch a startup that generates $1 million in revenue within two years."
2. *Why do you want to achieve it?* You need a compelling reason, something that sets your soul on fire and gives you the drive to push through the tough times. Instead of saying, "I want to make money," let's dig deeper. How about saying, "I want to create a product that solves a problem for millions of people and improves their lives"? Now, we're talking!
3. *How will you know when you have achieved it?* Be objective and realistic. Set benchmarks and milestones that track your progress and success. Let's get precise. Instead of saying, "I'll know it when I see it," say, "I'll measure my revenue, customer satisfaction, and market share every quarter, and adjust my strategy accordingly." That's the way to go!

Specificity: Breaking It Down into Actionable Steps

Now that we have clarity, it's time to roll up our sleeves and get specific. Specificity, the second essential element of a desire outcome, is like the GPS that guides you through the twists and turns of your journey. It's about breaking down your desired outcome into bite-sized, actionable steps. This way, you can avoid procrastination and overwhelm and stay on track to reach your destination.

To achieve specificity, we need to answer three pivotal questions:

1. *What are the actions that you need to take to achieve your desired outcome?* List the specific tasks, skills, and resources that you need to acquire, develop, or leverage. For example, if your desired outcome is to launch a startup, you need to conduct market research, develop a product, build a team, raise funds, and market your product. Get down to the specifics.
2. *What are the timelines and deadlines for each action?* Here comes the structure. Set specific and realistic deadlines for each task based on your available time, energy, and resources. Let's not leave it up to chance. For example, if you need to conduct market research, set a deadline of one month and break it down into smaller tasks such as defining your target audience, designing your survey, and analyzing your data. Now, you've got a roadmap!
3. *What are the potential obstacles and risks that you may face?* Life loves to throw curveballs, but we're ready for them! Anticipate the possible challenges and risks that may hinder your progress and develop contingency plans to tackle them head-on. For example, if you face a shortage of funds, you may explore alternative sources of funding such as crowdfunding or angel investors.

Meaning: Fueling Your Journey with Purpose

Last but certainly not least, let's talk about meaning. Meaning, the third essential element of a desired outcome, is the fuel that keeps you going when the going gets tough. It's about aligning your desired outcome with your values, passions, and strengths. When your journey has meaning, you'll find the motivation and resilience to overcome setbacks and failures along the way.

To achieve meaning, you need to answer these three fundamental questions:

1. *What are your core values?* These are the guiding principles that shape who you are and what you stand for. Integrity, compassion, creativity, justice—identify the values that drive your actions and decisions. Make sure your desired outcome reflects and honors these values. It's important to stay true to yourself.
2. *What are your passions?* We're not talking about those guilty pleasures like binge-watching your favorite TV show (though there's nothing wrong with that!). We're talking about the activities and interests that ignite your soul, bring you joy, excitement, and fulfillment. Find a way to weave your passions into your desired outcome. Let your journey be an expression of your true self!

3. *What are your strengths?* These are the things you're naturally good at. These are your secret weapons, your superpowers. Identify the skills, talents, and qualities that you excel at and enjoy using. Communication, problem-solving, leadership, empathy—embrace and leverage these strengths in pursuit of your desired outcome. You're a force to be reckoned with!

When your desired outcome has clarity, specificity, and meaning, it becomes a powerful and inspiring force that propels you toward success and fulfillment. You have a clear understanding of what you want to achieve, how you will achieve it, and why it matters to you. You have a detailed plan of action that breaks down your goal into manageable steps, timelines, and contingencies. And you have a deep connection to your values, passions, and strengths that fuels your motivation and resilience.

THE POWER OF DESIRE **WES BERRY**

Case Study: The Success Story: John F. Kennedy and NASA's Moon Landing

Now, let's take a moment to learn from the iconic success story of John F. Kennedy and NASA's moon landing. Talk about clarity, specificity, and meaning coming together!

In 1961, President Kennedy set the audacious goal of landing a human on the moon and returning them safely to Earth by the end of the decade. Now, that's what I call clarity and specificity! It was a mission that symbolized the technological prowess of the United States during the Cold War era—a goal with great meaning.

To achieve this monumental task, NASA developed a detailed plan of action that would make even the most organized among us swoon. They broke down the mission into manageable steps, timelines, and contingencies. It required the coordination of thousands of brilliant minds, the development of new technologies, and the unwavering commitment to the goal. Talk about specificity in action!

Despite facing setbacks and challenges, including the tragic loss of three astronauts, NASA remained resilient and focused on the desired outcome. On July 20, 1969, the world witnessed a giant leap for humankind when astronaut Neil Armstrong took that iconic step onto the lunar surface.

The success of the moon landing mission serves as a shining example of the power of clarity, specificity, and meaning. It shows us that with a clear vision, a detailed plan, and a deep sense of purpose, we can overcome any obstacle and achieve the extraordinary.

Conclusion

Achieving clarity, specificity, and meaning is not always easy. It requires self-awareness, reflection, and intentionality. It requires you to dig deep into your aspirations, values, and skills, and align them with your vision of success and fulfillment. It requires you to overcome the doubts, fears, and limiting beliefs that may hold you back and cultivate the courage, confidence, and growth mindset that will propel you forward. By answering the crucial questions of what, why, and how you'll bring your vision to life, you'll be able to prepare for the challenges that lie ahead. And don't forget to infuse your journey with passion!

Chapter 3

The Art of Goal-Setting: SMART Criteria and Beyond

Now, let's embark on a journey through the art of goal-setting, and let me tell you, it's a game-changer. If you want to achieve your desired outcomes, you gotta set some goals. Goals give you the roadmap, the fuel, and the kick in the pants you need to get there. Setting goals is like having a compass that guides you towards success. But it's not just about throwing darts in the dark; we need a strategic approach. That's where the SMART criteria come into play, along with some extra tips to take your goal-setting skills to the next level. So, grab a notebook, sharpen your pencils, and get ready to unleash your inner goal-setting guru!

SMART Criteria: The Superheroes of Goal-Setting
The SMART criteria are a popular framework for goal-setting, which stands for Specific, Measurable, Achievable, Relevant, and Time-bound. Each of these

criteria helps you create a goal that is clear, tangible, achievable and aligns with your overall vision and purpose.

Specific: Your goal needs to be as clear as it can be. It should answer the question of what exactly you want to achieve and how you'll get there. Avoid vague statements like "I want to lose weight." Instead, get specific and say something like, "I want to lose 10 pounds in 2 months by exercising for 30 minutes a day and following a balanced diet." See the difference? Specificity is key!

Measurable: If you can't measure it, you can't manage it. Your goal should be something you can track and quantify. This allows you to monitor your progress and make adjustments along the way. Rather than setting a goal like, "I want to be more productive," make it measurable by saying "I want to increase my productivity by 25% within a month by using a time-management app and eliminating distractions." Now you have a target to aim for!

Achievable: We all love a good challenge, but let's keep it real. Your goal should be something you believe you can actually achieve. It should push you out of your comfort zone without leaving you overwhelmed or demotivated. For instance, instead of setting an unrealistic goal like, "I want to become a millionaire overnight," set an achievable goal like, "I want to save $10,000 in a year by cutting back on expenses and investing wisely." Aim high, but keep it within reach!

Relevant: Your goal should matter to *you*. It should align with your values, passions, and long-term aspirations. Avoid setting goals just because they sound impressive. Instead, choose goals that resonate with you on a deep level. For example, rather than setting a goal like, "I want to learn a foreign language just for the sake of it," set a relevant goal like, "I want to learn Spanish because I plan to travel to South America and immerse myself in the local culture." Now you're getting personal!

Time-bound: Deadlines are your secret weapons. Your goal needs a specific timeframe to create a sense of urgency and focus. Rather than saying, "I want to write a book someday," set a time-bound goal like, "I want to write a 50,000-word book in 6 months by dedicating 2 hours a day to writing and seeking feedback from beta readers." Now you have a deadline to chase!

Beyond SMART Criteria: Unleash Your Inner Goal-Setting Guru

While SMART criteria provide a useful framework for goal-setting, they may not be sufficient for more complex or long-term goals. Here are some additional tips to enhance your goal-setting skills:

1. *Break down your goal into smaller milestones.* Instead of focusing only on the end result, break down your goal into smaller, achievable steps that you can celebrate along the way. For example, if your goal is to run a marathon, break it down into smaller milestones such as running a 5k, a 10k, a half-marathon, and finally, a full marathon.
2. *Create a vision board or a visual representation of your goal.* Use images, symbols, or words to represent your desired outcome, and display it in a prominent place where you can see it daily. This can help you stay motivated and inspired and visualize yourself achieving your goal.
3. *Share your goal with a supportive community or accountability partner.* Having a support network or someone to hold you accountable can increase your commitment and motivation to achieve your goal. Share your goal with a trusted friend, family member, or mentor, and ask them to check in with you regularly to see how you are progressing.
4. *Set a stretch goal or a BHAG (Big Hairy Audacious Goal).* While it's important to set achievable goals, it's also beneficial to set a goal that challenges you to push beyond your limits and explore new possibilities. A stretch goal or a BHAG can inspire you to think creatively, innovate, and achieve breakthrough results that you never thought were possible.

Continuously evaluate and adjust your goals. As you progress towards your goal, regularly evaluate your progress and adjust your approach if needed. Be open to feedback and learning, and be willing to pivot or change your strategy if you encounter obstacles or new opportunities.

Case Study: Usain Bolt

Let's look at the story of Usain Bolt, the world-renowned Jamaican sprinter who has won numerous Olympic and World Championship gold medals.

Bolt set multiple goals throughout his career, but one of his most notable was his goal to become the first person to run the 100-meter dash in under 9.5 seconds. He set this goal in 2008 after winning the gold medal in the 100-meter dash at the Beijing Olympics with a time of 9.69 seconds.

To achieve his goal, Bolt used the SMART criteria. He identified the specific goal of running the 100-meter dash in under 9.5 seconds, which was measurable and achievable based on his previous performances and physical abilities.

He also made the goal relevant to his career aspirations and set a time-bound deadline to achieve it.

Bolt's training regimen was also specifically designed to help him achieve this goal. He worked with his coach and support team to develop a training plan that focused on his speed, technique, and endurance and included strength training, flexibility exercises, and recovery practices.

In August 2009, Bolt achieved his goal at the World Championships in Berlin, Germany, when he ran the 100-meter dash in 9.58 seconds, setting a new world record. His use of the SMART criteria and effective training plan were key factors in his success.

The story of Usain Bolt demonstrates how effective goal-setting, combined with a clear plan of action and dedicated effort, can help individuals achieve remarkable feats and reach their full potential.

Conclusion

Setting goals is a powerful tool for achieving success and fulfillment in life. By using the SMART criteria and other goal-setting tips, you can create goals that are clear and meaningful and increase your chances of achieving them. Remember to stay committed, motivated, and flexible, and celebrate your progress and success along the way.

Chapter 4

The Science of Motivation: Intrinsic vs. Extrinsic Drivers

Ah, motivation - the holy grail of achieving our wildest dreams. It's the spark that lights the fire under us and propels us towards our desired outcomes. But motivation is no easy ride. There are all sorts of factors at play, from our beliefs and values to our basic human needs and the promise of rewards. In this chapter, we will dive into the nitty-gritty of what makes us tick and the difference between those intrinsic and extrinsic drivers. Let's unravel the science of motivation!

Intrinsic Motivation

Intrinsic motivation refers to the internal drive to pursue a task or goal because it is inherently enjoyable, interesting, or meaningful to us. Intrinsic motivation is fueled by the satisfaction, pleasure, and sense of accomplishment that comes from the activity itself rather than external rewards or pressure. Think of it as that burning passion within you that fuels your inner fire. Examples of intrinsic motivation include pursuing a hobby, reading a book for pleasure, or volunteering for a cause that aligns with one's values.

Research has shown that intrinsic motivation is associated with higher levels of engagement, creativity, persistence, and satisfaction compared to extrinsic motivation. Intrinsic motivation promotes a sense of autonomy, competence, and relatedness, which are essential for human well-being and thriving. When we are intrinsically motivated, we feel in control of our actions, confident in our abilities, and connected to others who share our interests and values.

So, how do you foster intrinsic motivation? Well, it's all about aligning your goals and activities with your passions, interests, and values. Seek out activities that challenge you, provide opportunities for growth and learning, and allow you to express your authentic self. Create a supportive environment that nurtures your intrinsic motivation by seeking feedback and social support and reframing failures as opportunities for growth.

Extrinsic Motivation

Extrinsic motivation refers to the *external* incentives or pressures that drive us to pursue a task or goal. Extrinsic motivation comes in various forms, like rewards, recognition, praise, grades, or even punishments. It's all about the desire to obtain a tangible or intangible outcome, whether it's money, status, approval, or avoiding negative consequences.

Examples of extrinsic motivation include working overtime to earn a bonus, studying hard to get a good grade, or complying with a rule to avoid a fine.

Research has shown that extrinsic motivation can be effective in initiating and sustaining behaviors, particularly in contexts where the task or goal is not inherently interesting or enjoyable. However, extrinsic motivation can also undermine intrinsic motivation and lead to negative outcomes, such as decreased creativity, engagement, and satisfaction. Excessive use of extrinsic rewards or punishment can also create a dependence on external sources of motivation and reduce one's sense of autonomy and intrinsic motivation.

To use extrinsic motivation effectively, it is important to balance it with intrinsic motivation and create a supportive environment that encourages autonomy, competence, and relatedness. Extrinsic motivation should be used as a complement to, rather than a substitute for, intrinsic motivation. For example, rewards should be used to recognize and reinforce desirable behaviors rather than as a bribe or a way to control behavior. Punishments should be used sparingly and as a last resort, and preferably, should be accompanied by explanations and opportunities for corrective action.

Practical Exercise: Discovering Your Intrinsic Motivations

Now, let's get practical and discover your intrinsic motivations. Here's a little exercise for you:

Reflect on your passions, interests, and values. What activities do you enjoy doing for their own sake? What topics or issues do you care about deeply? What are your core values and beliefs?

Identify the activities or goals that give you a sense of satisfaction, enjoyment, or accomplishment. These may be related to your work, hobbies, or personal life.

Explore ways to align your goals and activities with your passions, interests, and values. Can you find ways to incorporate your passions into your work or daily life? Can you set goals that challenge you and allow you to express your authentic self?

Case Study: The Google 20% Time

Google, the tech giant known for its innovative and creative culture, has a unique program called "20% time," which allows its employees to spend 20% of their work time pursuing their own projects and ideas. The program was introduced in 2004 and has since been credited with many of Google's successful products, such as Gmail, Google News, and Google Maps.

The 20%-time program is an example of intrinsic motivation, as it allows employees to pursue their own passions, interests, and goals without external pressures or rewards. It aligns with Google's values of autonomy, creativity, and innovation and has been shown to increase employee engagement, productivity, and job satisfaction.

The 20%-time program also demonstrates the importance of creating a supportive environment that nurtures intrinsic motivation. Google provides its employees with resources, feedback, and mentorship to help them pursue their projects and encourages collaboration and sharing of ideas. The program has also been used as a recruiting tool, as it attracts talented individuals who value autonomy and creativity.

Conclusion

Motivation is the secret sauce to achieving your dreams. Create a supportive environment that nurtures your intrinsic motivation. Seek feedback and support from others who share your interests and values. Surround yourself with positive and inspiring people and resources. By understanding the difference between intrinsic and extrinsic motivation, and nurturing your inner fire, you can harness the power within you to propel yourself forward.

Chapter 5

The Role of Values, Purpose, and Identity in Desired Outcomes

Now, let's get down to business, shall we? If we want to achieve our desired outcomes, we can't ignore the powerhouse trio of our values, purpose, and identity. These three elements play a crucial role in providing us with direction, meaning, and authenticity. And let's face it, when we're living in alignment with our true selves, that's when the real magic happens. So, in this chapter, we'll be taking a closer look at these three key components and how they can shape the path towards our desired outcomes. Get ready to dive in!

Values

Values are the fundamental principles, beliefs, and priorities that guide our actions, decisions, and behaviors. Our values reflect what we consider important, worthwhile, and meaningful in life, and they influence our attitudes, emotions, and goals. Some common values include honesty, respect, kindness, justice, creativity, and growth.

Research has shown that when we align our goals and behaviors with our values, we experience greater well-being, motivation, and satisfaction. On the other hand, when we violate our values or engage in behaviors that conflict with them, we experience negative emotions, guilt, and cognitive dissonance.

So, how do we uncover our values? You'll need to do a little soul-searching. Reflect on what truly matters to you in life. What gets your engine revving? What do you stand for? And take a peek at your role models, heroes, or even those people you secretly follow on social media (don't worry, we won't judge). What qualities do they embody? Once you've identified your values, use them to navigate the ups and downs of life. They'll help you make decisions, take action, and build meaningful relationships.

Purpose

Purpose is the sense of direction, meaning, and contribution that gives our lives a sense of significance and fulfillment. It's like the GPS system that keeps us on track and motivated. Purpose is the answer to the question "why" we do what we do, and it provides us with a sense of motivation, focus, and resilience. Purpose can also help us overcome obstacles, setbacks, and challenges, as we see them as opportunities for growth and learning. It can enhance our creativity and problem-solving abilities as we approach tasks with a sense of mission and passion, and purpose is even associated with greater well-being, resilience, and longevity. Purpose can also enhance our creativity, innovation, and problem-solving abilities as we approach tasks with a sense of mission and passion.

So, how do we find our purpose? Start by reflecting on what brings you joy, satisfaction, and a sense of accomplishment. You can also consider what problems or issues you care deeply about and how you can contribute to their solutions. Don't forget to tap into your values, strengths, and talents. How can they be used to positively impact the world? Embrace that sense of mission and passion, and let purpose be the fuel that propels you towards your desired outcomes.

Identity

Identity is the unique blend of beliefs, values, and characteristics that define who we are and how we see ourselves. Identity comes in many flavors, from our gender, ethnicity, and culture to our occupation, hobbies, and personality traits. It influences our attitudes, behaviors, and relationships, and it adds that special touch of belonging, self-esteem, and purpose. Identity can also provide us with a sense of connection, pride, and inspiration as we see ourselves as part of a larger group or community.

But here's the thing: to develop a positive identity, you need to cultivate it with care. Embracing your strengths, values, and unique qualities and celebrating your successes and accomplishments is essential. You can also seek support and validation from others who share your identity and participate in activities or groups that reflect your identity.

However, it is also important to recognize and challenge any negative stereotypes, biases, or limitations associated with your identity and cultivate a sense of openness, curiosity, and empathy towards others with different identities.

Practical Exercise: Values, Purpose, and Identity Reflection

To apply the concepts of values, purpose, and identity to your own life, you can use the following exercise:

- *Values:* Write down your top 5-10 values, and reflect on how they influence your decisions, actions, and relationships. Ask yourself if you are living according to your values or if there are any areas where you need to align your behavior with your values.
- *Purpose:* Write down your life sense of purpose or mission, and reflect on how it motivates and guides you. Ask yourself if your current activities and goals are aligned with your purpose or if there are any changes you need to make to pursue your purpose more effectively.
- *Identity:* Write down your identity or sense of self, and reflect on how it influences your attitudes, behaviors, and relationships. Ask yourself if your identity is empowering or limiting you and if you need to challenge or overcome any stereotypes, biases, or limitations.

Case Study: Elon Musk's Purpose and Identity

Elon Musk, the billionaire entrepreneur known for his ambitious and innovative projects, such as SpaceX and Tesla, has a clear sense of purpose and identity that has guided his success.

Musk's purpose is to advance humanity and make life multi-planetary, as he believes that the survival and progress of humanity depend on becoming a space-faring civilization. His identity is that of a visionary, risk-taker, and problem-solver who is not afraid to challenge conventional wisdom and push the boundaries of science and technology.

Musk's purpose and identity have influenced his desired outcomes, as he has set ambitious goals for his companies, such as launching rockets, landing them back on Earth, and developing electric cars that are affordable and sustainable. Musk's purpose and identity have also shaped his leadership style, as he encourages his employees to embrace his vision and take risks, and he is willing to invest his own money and reputation in his projects.

However, Musk's purpose and identity have also been challenged by setbacks, controversies, and criticism. For example, Musk's tweets and public statements have been criticized for their impulsivity, inaccuracies, and insensitivity. Musk has also faced legal and ethical issues, such as allegations of labor violations, safety concerns, and conflicts of interest.

Despite these challenges, Musk's purpose and identity have remained strong as he continues to pursue his goals and inspire others to join him. Musk's purpose and identity can serve as an example of how a clear and inspiring vision, combined with a strong sense of self and values, can lead to remarkable outcomes and impact.

Conclusion

By reflecting on your values, purpose, and identity, you can gain clarity and direction in your desired outcomes, and increase your motivation, resilience, and satisfaction. Seek feedback and support from others who share your values, purpose, and identity. Learn from their experiences and perspectives. And remember, it's your unique blend of values, purpose, and identity that will make you stand out in the crowd.

Chapter 6

The Power Trio: Visualization, Affirmation, and Meditation

Alright, I know, at first these ideas sounded kooky to me too. But when it comes to achieving our desired outcomes, it's not just about taking external actions and making plans. We also need to tap into the power of our internal mental and emotional states. That's why, in this chapter, we're going to explore the importance of visualization, affirmation, and meditation. Trust me, these techniques can work wonders when it comes to boosting our motivation, focus, and resilience.

Visualization – Seeing is Achieving

Visualization is the process of creating mental images of our desired outcomes as if they have already happened. Visualization can help us clarify our goals, boost our motivation, and enhance our confidence and self-efficacy. It can also activate our subconscious mind, which can influence our thoughts, emotions, and behaviors.

Research has shown that visualization can improve performance in various domains, such as sports, music, and business. For example, a study by the University of Chicago found that basketball players who visualized making free throws had a higher success rate than those who did not. Another study by the University of Plymouth found that musicians who visualized playing their instruments had better accuracy and timing than those who did not.

So, how can you incorporate visualization into your life? It's simple. Start by creating a clear and vivid mental image of your desired outcome using all your senses. You can imagine yourself in the situation, feeling confident, capable, and successful. You can also use visualization to overcome obstacles and challenges by imagining yourself finding solutions and learning from mistakes. It's like creating your very own blockbuster movie, starring none other than yourself!

Affirmation – Talk Yourself Up

Affirmation is the process of using positive self-talk and language to reinforce our beliefs, values, and goals. It's a powerful tool! An affirmation can help us overcome negative self-talk, self-doubt, and limiting beliefs and replace them with positive and empowering messages. An affirmation can also enhance our self-esteem, self-awareness, and self-acceptance.

Affirmations can improve performance, reduce stress, and enhance well-being. A study by the University of Pennsylvania found that students who practiced self-affirmation had better academic performance and reduced stress levels. Another study by the University of California found that affirmations improved self-esteem and reduced symptoms of depression in breast cancer patients.

To use affirmations, identify your core beliefs, values, and goals. Create positive statements that reflect them. Use present tense statements like, "I am confident," "I am worthy," or "I am successful." Tailor your affirmations to your desired outcome. Say things like, "I am getting closer to my goal every day" or "I have the skills and resources to achieve my goal." Repeat them like a mantra, and watch the magic unfold.

Meditation- Zen and the Art of Success

Now, I can already hear some of you saying, "Meditation? That's for yogis and gurus, right?" Well, my friends, meditation is not just for the enlightened. It's for everyone who wants to find their inner peace and achieve their desired outcomes.

Meditation is the practice of focusing your attention on a specific object, such as your breath, a mantra, or a visualization. It helps to reduce stress, increase mindfulness, and enhance our cognitive and emotional control. Meditation can also improve our self-awareness, empathy, and compassion.

Meditation can improve various aspects of our physical and mental health, such as reducing anxiety and depression, improving sleep quality, and enhancing cognitive function. In a study by the University of California, researchers found that meditation improved working memory and attention in adults. Another study by Harvard Medical School found that meditation reduced symptoms of anxiety and depression in patients with chronic pain.

To start your meditation practice, find a quiet and comfortable place where you can sit or lie down. Close your eyes and choose a specific object of focus, whether it's your breath, a mantra, or a visualization. Let your mind settle and gently bring your attention back to your chosen focus whenever it wanders. Start with just a few minutes of meditation per day and gradually increase the duration and frequency. It's like giving your mind a mini vacation.

The power of visualization lies in its ability to make the intangible, tangible.

Case Study: Oprah Winfrey's Visualization, Affirmation, and Meditation

Oprah Winfrey, one of the most successful and influential media personalities in the world, has often attributed her success to the power of visualization, affirmation, and meditation. In her book, *The Wisdom of Sundays*, Oprah shares her daily practice of visualizing and affirming her goals, as well as meditating to enhance her focus and clarity.

Oprah incorporates visualization into her daily practice by creating mental images of her desired outcomes. Whether it's completing a project, delivering a speech, or achieving a personal goal, she sees herself succeeding. She visualizes overcoming obstacles and challenges, and she learns from her mistakes along the way. It's like she's directing her own blockbuster life story.

When it comes to affirmation, Oprah knows how to talk herself up. She reinforces her beliefs, values, and goals through positive self-talk. One of her favorite affirmations is, "I trust myself," a reminder of her own power and capability. She replaces self-doubt with self-confidence, and fear with faith. It's like she's her own personal cheerleader.

And let's not forget about meditation. Oprah practices transcendental meditation, a technique that involves using a mantra to focus the mind and achieve deep relaxation. She meditates twice a day, for 20 minutes each session. Meditation enhances her mental clarity, creativity, and compassion. It's like she's finding her Zen amidst the chaos of her busy life.

Oprah's example shows us how the combination of visualization, affirmation, and meditation can lead to remarkable success. By cultivating a positive and focused internal state, we can enhance our external actions and strategies. We can create a fulfilling and successful life, no matter what our desired outcomes may be.

Conclusion

These powerful techniques clarify our goals, boost our motivation, and enhance our self-confidence and self-efficacy. They help us overcome negative self-talk, self-doubt, and limiting beliefs. They reduce stress, increase mindfulness, and enhance our cognitive and emotional control. By incorporating visualization, affirmation, and meditation into our daily routine, we can create a life that is fulfilling and successful, whatever our desired outcomes may be.

It's time to unleash the power of your mind. See your success, speak your truth, and find your inner calm. The magic is within you. It's time to create the life you've always dreamed of.

Get ready to unlock your brain's full potential!

Chapter 7

The Cognitive Skills, Abilities, and Intuitive Thinking that Drive Success

Have you ever had a feeling about something, even when you didn't have all the facts? Or maybe you've noticed patterns in your daily routine, like your mood or productivity, that help you plan your day like a pro. Heck, if you're an entrepreneur, you might've even spotted a gap in the market for a new product or service. These are all examples of the cognitive processes that are vital to our daily lives and can drive success in various domains.

So, in this chapter, we're going to dig into three of these processes: pattern recognition, perceptual completion, and opportunity recognition. And we're not just going to stop there. I'm going give you the skills you need to develop these processes and achieve tremendous success and fulfillment. Get ready to unlock your brain's full potential!

Pattern Recognition - Unleashing the Sherlock Holmes Within

Pattern recognition is the ability to detect regularities or patterns in data and use these patterns to predict future outcomes. This cognitive process is essential in many domains, such as business, finance, and sports, where identifying trends or patterns can help to make better decisions and gain a competitive advantage.

For instance, a sales manager who notices sales increase during a specific time of year can adjust their marketing and sales strategies accordingly to capitalize on this pattern. Similarly, financial analysts use pattern recognition to identify market trends and predict future stock prices.

Pattern recognition isn't just about business. It's a fundamental cognitive process that underlies many other skills, like language acquisition, music perception, and even face recognition. Babies learn language by detecting patterns in the sounds they hear, and musicians rely on pattern recognition to groove to the beats. It's like our brains are wired to be pattern detectives!

Perceptual Completion - Filling in the Blanks, Picasso-Style

Perceptual completion is the brain's version of Picasso's art. It's filling in missing information based on context and past experiences. This skill is essential when dealing with sensory information that is incomplete or ambiguous.

Imagine you're looking at a picture with part of it hidden behind a curtain. You can only see a fraction of the image, but your brain automatically fills in the missing information based on your past experiences and the context. Voila! You perceive the object as a whole. It's like your brain is an artistic genius, painting the missing details to complete the masterpiece.

Perceptual completion is not just about visual perception. It's also crucial in social interactions. Think about it. When you see someone's facial expressions or body language, you're not just looking at isolated features. Your brain fills in the missing information based on contextual cues and past experiences, allowing you to understand the emotions and intentions of others. It's like having a sixth sense for decoding social signals.

Opportunity Recognition - Unleashing the Entrepreneurial Spirit

Opportunity recognition involves identifying potential opportunities or connections that might lead to future benefits. This skill is particularly important in entrepreneurship, where identifying opportunities can lead to creating new products or services and, ultimately, business success.

Let's say you're an entrepreneur with a keen eye for spotting opportunities. You notice a gap in the market for a new type of technology, and boom! Your entrepreneurial brain starts buzzing with ideas. You create a new product or service that meets this need, and before you know it, you've gained a competitive advantage in the market. Opportunity recognition is like having a secret radar that detects hidden gems in the business world.

Related Skills - Unleashing Your Inner Superhero

Pattern recognition, perceptual completion, and opportunity recognition are complex cognitive processes that involve multiple skills and abilities. Here are some of the related skills that can help you develop these cognitive processes and succeed in various domains:

- *Creativity* is closely linked to pattern recognition and opportunity recognition, as it involves approaching problems from multiple angles and considering a range of possibilities. Creative thinking can also help overcome mental blocks or biases that might prevent us from recognizing patterns or opportunities.
- *Critical thinking* is essential for making well-informed decisions and judgments based on the patterns and opportunities we recognize. It involves analyzing and evaluating evidence, questioning assumptions, and considering multiple perspectives.
- *Attention to detail* is critical for pattern recognition and perceptual completion, as it involves noticing and analyzing small facts and differences that others might overlook. This skill also requires a high level of focus and concentration.

- *Open-mindedness* is crucial for recognizing opportunities that might not be immediately obvious. It involves considering and exploring new ideas and perspectives, even if they challenge our preconceptions.
- *Adaptability* is essential for responding to new opportunities and challenges. It involves adjusting to new situations, changing circumstances, and being open to new approaches and strategies.

Intuitive Thinking

Another skill that is closely related to pattern recognition, perceptual completion, and opportunity recognition is intuitive thinking. It's like a sixth sense, or a hunch. Intuitive thinking makes quick and accurate judgments based on limited information or past experiences. This skill can be particularly useful in situations where there is a high degree of uncertainty or ambiguity.

For example, imagine you are a doctor who needs to diagnose a patient with a rare and complex condition. By relying on your past experiences and knowledge, you might be able to make an accurate diagnosis based on limited information.

Intuitive thinking can also be helpful in business and entrepreneurship, where quick decisions and accurate judgments are essential. By developing intuitive thinking skills, entrepreneurs can make rapid and informed decisions that can help them stay ahead of the competition and identify new opportunities.

However, it is essential to note that intuitive thinking is not a substitute for critical thinking or careful analysis. While intuitive thinking can be a valuable tool, it should be used with other cognitive processes to ensure that decisions are based on sound reasoning and evidence.

Developing Your Cognitive Skills and Abilities

Now that you know the secrets of pattern recognition, perceptual completion, opportunity recognition, and the related skills, it's time to unleash your inner superhero. Here are some strategies to develop and strengthen your cognitive powers:

- *Practice identifying patterns:* One way to improve your pattern recognition skills is to look for patterns in your daily life activities, such as your work or school assignments, your routines, or your social interactions. By practicing pattern recognition, you can train your brain to detect regularities and use them to make predictions and informed decisions.
- *Expose yourself to new experiences:* Expand your horizons and expose yourself to new and unfamiliar experiences. By stepping out of your comfort zone, you can develop a more diverse set of past experiences to draw upon when filling in missing information. So, try new

things, meet new people, and embrace the unknown. By experiencing new contexts and situations, you can develop a more robust set of past experiences when filling in the missing information.

- *Stay informed and curious:* Knowledge is power. To improve your opportunity recognition skills, stay knowledgeable about changes and trends in your industry or field. Read news articles, attend conferences, and talk to experts to stay up to date on the latest developments. Curiosity and a willingness to explore new ideas can help you identify opportunities others might overlook.

- *Trust your instincts:* Sometimes, your gut feeling can be your greatest asset. Practice trusting your instincts and making quick judgments based on limited information. But remember, balance your intuition with critical thinking and careful analysis to ensure your decisions are grounded in evidence and reasoning. Trust your instincts, but also trust your brain.

- *Seek feedback and seek to improve:* Finally, seek feedback from others and be open to constructive criticism. Use feedback to identify areas where you can improve your cognitive skills and abilities and consciously address any weaknesses. Embrace a growth mindset and never stop learning and evolving.

Case Study: Albert Einstein

Albert Einstein is widely regarded as one of the most brilliant minds in history. His contributions to physics revolutionized our understanding of the universe and paved the way for numerous scientific advancements. But what made Einstein such a remarkable thinker? Let's take a closer look at the cognitive skills, abilities, and intuitive thinking that drove his success.

Cognitive Skills and Abilities

Einstein possessed exceptional spatial reasoning skills, allowing him to visualize complex shapes and patterns in his mind. This ability helped him conceptualize and solve some of the most challenging physics problems of his time. His brain was like a 3D printer, constructing intricate models of the universe.

In addition to his spatial reasoning, Einstein had an exceptional memory. He could recall complex equations and formulas with ease, often reciting them from memory without the aid of notes or textbooks. This remarkable memory allowed him to access the information he needed to solve problems and make connections between seemingly unrelated concepts. It's like he had a vast library in his brain, ready to be accessed at any moment.

Intuitive Thinking

But it wasn't just his cognitive abilities that set Einstein apart. It was his intuitive thinking. Einstein had the courage to challenge established theories and beliefs, relying on his intuition to guide his scientific inquiry. His intuition led him to develop the theory of relativity, which revolutionized our understanding of time and space. Einstein realized that the laws of physics were the same for all observers, regardless of their relative motion. This led him to develop a new theory of time and space, which challenged the widely accepted Newtonian view of the universe. He could see well beyond the constraints of conventional thinking.

Einstein's intuitive thinking led him to make numerous groundbreaking discoveries throughout his career. From his understanding of the dual nature of light to his work on the photoelectric effect, his ability to think intuitively allowed him to push the boundaries of science. He wasn't afraid to follow his instincts and explore uncharted territories. His intuition was like a compass that pointed him in the direction of scientific greatness.

Although he received the Nobel Prize in Physics in 1921, Einstein's intuitive thinking was not always well-received by the scientific community. His ideas often challenged existing theories and beliefs, and many scientists were skeptical of his unconventional approach. However, Einstein remained steadfast in his convictions, relying on his intuition to guide him even in the face of criticism and opposition.

Albert Einstein's success can be attributed to his exceptional cognitive skills and abilities, as well as his intuitive thinking. His strong spatial reasoning skills, exceptional memory, and analytical mind allowed him to approach complex problems with ease, while his intuitive thinking allowed him to make groundbreaking discoveries that challenged the status quo. Einstein's approach to science was unconventional, but his willingness to follow his intuition and think outside the box led to some of the most significant scientific discoveries of the 20th century. His legacy continues to inspire and influence scientists and thinkers around the world, making him one of the most important figures in the history of science.

Conclusion

You now have the keys to unlock the full potential of your amazing brain. Pattern recognition, perceptual completion, opportunity recognition, and intuitive thinking are essential cognitive skills and abilities that can drive success in various domains. These are tricky subjects and can be easily confused. Developing the related skills of creativity, critical thinking, attention to detail, open-mindedness, and adaptability can help us hone these processes and achieve greater success and fulfillment in our personal and professional lives. We can gain a competitive advantage and achieve our goals by improving our ability to recognize patterns, fill in missing information, identify potential opportunities, and make quick and accurate judgments. By developing these cognitive processes and honing their related skills, you can become the superhero you were always meant to be.

Positive thinking can lead to success in many areas of life, including relationships, career, and personal growth.

Chapter 8

Positive Thinking: Unlocking Your Path to Success and Happiness

If you've been hanging around the self-help section of the bookstore, you've probably come across the idea of positive thinking. Even Henry Ford has been quoted as saying, "Whether you think you can or you think you can't you're right." The notion that what we think and how we feel can make or break our dreams has been around for ages. In this chapter, we'll take a closer look at how a positive outlook can help us achieve our heart's desires and make life a little sweeter.

Firstly, positive thinking can be defined as the practice of focusing on the good things in life rather than dwelling on the negative. It involves cultivating a mindset that is optimistic, hopeful, and proactive. This type of thinking can lead to success in many areas of life, including relationships, career, and personal growth.

But what does science have to say about it? Well, research has shown that positive thinking has a significant impact on our physical and mental health. In a fascinating study published in the

Journal of Personality and Social Psychology, it was discovered that people with a positive outlook on life tend to have better physical health, experience less stress, and even live longer than those with a negative mindset. Yes, you heard that right—positive thinking can add some precious years to our lives! This is because positive thinking can help reduce the production of stress hormones, such as cortisol, and promote the production of feel-good chemicals, such as dopamine and serotonin.

In addition to its impact on health, positive thinking can also lead to success in relationships. Research has shown that people who have a positive outlook are more likely to attract positive people into their lives and have better relationships with others. This is because positive thinking can help us be more open-minded, empathetic, and compassionate towards others, which can create stronger connections and foster greater trust and understanding.

Positive thinking can also be a key factor in career success, a literal game-changer in the workplace. A study published in the *Journal of Applied Psychology* found that people who have a positive outlook on their work are more likely to have better job satisfaction, perform better, and be more resilient in the face of challenges. This is because positive thinking can help us be more motivated, creative, and proactive, which can lead to greater success in our careers.

But the benefits of positive thinking don't stop there. It can also be a mighty tool for personal growth and development.

Positive thinking fosters a growth-oriented mindset that helps us learn from our mistakes, develop new skills, and embrace challenges. Our positive thoughts propel us forward on our journey of self-improvement. When we adopt a positive mindset, we become more open to new experiences and view failure as an opportunity for growth and learning. It's like having a compass that guides us toward becoming the best version of ourselves.

So with all of this good news about positive thinking, what if we aren't naturally a positive thinker? Or what if we've had so many bad things happen, that our attitude has turned negative? How do we become a positive thinking person?

Here are a few suggestions to get you started:

- *Notice your thinking patterns.* You might not even be aware of them. If you are stuck in traffic, do you start thinking how late it will make you to work, then how behind you are going to get, and how upset your boss will be and suddenly you've ruined your entire day before it barely starts?
- *Reframe your thoughts.* This is probably the most important step. When you catch yourself thinking negatively, try to reframe it. Instead of "Oh man, he's going to be so angry that I'm late and I might get fired or get passed up for that promotion . . ." think , "Yes, now I'm

going to be a few minutes late, but it can't be helped. There was an accident on the freeway. My boss will understand. I hope the people in the accident didn't get hurt badly. I'm so thankful it wasn't me in that accident." It sounds hokey, but it works. Your mind can trick your body into relaxing, and you'll avoid those hunched shoulders and tense muscles that would otherwise make you arrive at work with a headache.

- *Give grace to yourself and to others.* You tried your best to be on time. Tomorrow, you can get up a few minutes earlier and check the traffic. You can listen attentively to your boss if he or she is angry with you, and realize that they too have deadlines to meet. We all have things going on, and most of us are doing the best we can do at the moment.
- *Laugh more.* This is the best de-stressor and a great way to frame your positive thinking. If you spill coffee on your white shirt before the meeting, try to find the humor in it. I love making jokes, and while sometimes it is inappropriate to joke, most of the time laughter dispels any tension in the room. Laughter, after all, is the best medicine.

Overall, the evidence suggests that positive thinking can have a significant impact on our lives and our success in achieving our desires. By focusing on the good things in life and cultivating an optimistic, hopeful, and proactive mindset, we can improve our physical and mental health, strengthen our relationships, enhance our career success, and foster personal growth and development.

Case Study: Ellen DeGeneres

Ellen DeGeneres is a well-known television host, comedian, and actress who has achieved significant success in her career. Throughout her life and career, DeGeneres has been known for her positive attitude and optimistic outlook. Her success can be attributed in part to her use of positive thinking and the impact it has had on her life.

Ellen is not just a strong advocate for positivity; she embodies it in everything she does. She firmly believes that positivity is the key to success, and she encourages her viewers to adopt a positive attitude in their own lives. Just take a look at her popular talk show, *The Ellen DeGeneres Show*, which features uplifting and inspiring stories that promote positive thinking and kindness. Ellen knows that positivity has the power to make a real difference, and she uses her platform to spread joy and positivity to millions of people.

But Ellen's journey hasn't been without its challenges. She faced the daunting task of coming out as a lesbian in the public eye, and she encountered numerous obstacles along the way. However, Ellen's positive mindset never wavered. Her unwavering optimism and resilience allowed her to overcome those obstacles and achieve remarkable success. With 30 Emmys under her belt and a highly successful career spanning over a decade, Ellen is a true testament to the power of positive thinking.

But Ellen's story doesn't end with career success. She is also renowned for her philanthropic work and her commitment to giving back. Ellen's positivity and desire to make a difference in the world have led her to support various charities and causes that are close to her heart. She uses her platform to raise awareness for issues such as animal rights and LGBTQ+ rights and has donated millions of dollars to charitable organizations. Ellen is proof that positive thinking not only brings personal success but also allows us to make a positive impact on the world around us.

Conclusion

Positive thinking is a powerful concept that can have a significant impact on our lives and success in achieving our desires. By cultivating an optimistic, hopeful, and proactive mindset, we can improve our physical and mental health, strengthen our relationships, enhance our career success, and foster personal growth and development. The evidence suggests that positive thinking can help us live longer, experience less stress, have better relationships, perform better in our careers, and be more open to new experiences and opportunities for growth.

So, let's embrace the power of positive thinking in our daily lives. Let's focus on the good things, radiate positivity, and approach challenges with optimism. Remember, positive thinking is like a magic wand that can unlock your path to success and happiness. So, go forth and conquer the world with a smile on your face and a positive mindset in your heart. The possibilities are endless!

PART 2
Pursue Your Desire

"When you have a dream that you can't let go of, trust your instincts and pursue it. But remember: Real dreams take work, they take patience, and sometimes they require you to dig down very deep. Be sure you're willing to do that."
Harvey Mackay

In the fast-paced and ever-changing landscape of business, it's crucial to stay ahead of the game and be prepared to adapt at a moment's notice.

Chapter 9

Mapping Your Terrain: PESTLE Analysis and Environmental Scanning

If you want to make it in the business world, you better be ready to hustle! In this fast-paced and ever-changing landscape, it's crucial to stay ahead of the game and be prepared to adapt at a moment's notice. And to do that, you gotta know what's going on outside your bubble. That's where environmental scanning comes in—it's like having a crystal ball that shows you what's coming your way. And what better crystal ball than the PESTLE framework? It's got everything you need to know about Political, Economic, Sociocultural, Technological, Legal, and Environmental factors. So buckle up, and let's dive in to map out your business terrain!

What in the World Is PESTLE Analysis?

PESTLE analysis is a strategic tool used to identify and analyze the external factors that affect an organization. It is a framework that consists of six key factors: Political, Economic, Sociocultural, Technological, Legal, and Environmental. By examining each of these factors, businesses can gain a deeper understanding of the external environment and the potential impact it may have on their operations.

Political Factors: Political factors refer to the government policies and regulations that can impact businesses. This includes taxation policies, trade restrictions, employment laws, and other factors that may affect the business environment. For example, changes in tax laws can have a significant impact on a business's profitability, while changes in trade regulations can affect the availability of goods and services.

Economic Factors: Economic factors refer to the broader economic conditions that may impact a business. This includes factors such as inflation, exchange rates, interest rates, and economic growth rates. Changes in economic conditions can have a significant impact on a business's revenue and profitability, as well as the availability of financing and resources.

Sociocultural Factors: Sociocultural factors refer to the social and cultural factors that may impact a business. This includes factors such as demographic changes, consumer attitudes, and lifestyle trends. Sociocultural factors can have a significant impact on consumer behavior and the demand for products and services.

Technological Factors: Technological factors refer to the advancements in technology that may impact a business. This includes factors such as automation, artificial intelligence, and the internet of things. Technological advancements can create new opportunities for businesses, but they can also create new challenges and disrupt traditional business models.

Legal Factors: Legal factors refer to the laws and regulations that may impact a business. This includes factors such as consumer protection laws, employment laws, and intellectual property laws. Changes in legal regulations can have a significant impact on a business's operations and may require changes to business practices.

Environmental Factors: Environmental factors refer to the physical environment in which a business operates. This includes factors such as climate change, natural disasters, and resource depletion. Environmental factors can have a significant impact on a business's operations and may require changes to business practices to ensure sustainability.

Conducting a PESTLE Analysis:
Now that we've explored the PESTLE factors, it's time to chart your course through the business terrain. How, you ask? By conducting a PESTLE analysis.

Start by identifying the key factors that may impact your operations. Gather your team, brainstorm, and conduct research to understand the external environment. Once you've identified these factors, evaluate their potential impact and level of importance.

Remember, external factors may be beyond our control, but by identifying threats and opportunities, we can develop strategies to mitigate risk and take advantage of opportunities. A well-conducted PESTLE analysis serves as your compass, guiding you through the stormy waters of the business world.

Using PESTLE Analysis to Map Your Business Terrain:

Once your PESTLE analysis is complete, it's time to utilize the insights gained to map your business terrain. Develop strategies to address the threats and opportunities presented by the external environment that you found. If political instability threatens a key market, consider diversifying your operations or building relationships with influential political stakeholders. If a technological breakthrough creates an opportunity for growth, invest in research and development to seize the moment.

Remember, environmental scanning is an ongoing process. The external environment is ever-changing, like a tempestuous sea. Regularly conduct PESTLE analyses, update your strategies, and remain vigilant. By doing so, you'll stay ahead of the curve, navigate the terrain with finesse, and maintain your competitive edge.

Benefits of PESTLE Analysis and Environmental Scanning

There are several benefits to conducting a PESTLE analysis and environmental scanning. These include:

Strategic Planning: PESTLE analysis and environmental scanning can provide valuable insights for strategic planning. By identifying key external factors that may impact the organization, businesses can develop strategies to mitigate risk and take advantage of opportunities.

Risk Management: PESTLE analysis and environmental scanning can help businesses identify potential threats and take steps to manage them. This can help reduce the impact of external factors on the organization's operations.

Competitive Advantage: By staying ahead of the curve and identifying new opportunities before competitors, businesses can gain a competitive advantage in the marketplace.

Innovation: PESTLE analysis and environmental scanning can help businesses identify new trends and technologies that may present opportunities for innovation and growth.

Flexibility: By regularly conducting PESTLE analysis and environmental scanning, businesses can remain flexible and adapt quickly to changes in the external environment.

Case Study: Tesla's Environmental Scanning

Tesla is a global electric vehicle and renewable energy company that has disrupted the automotive and energy industries. Tesla's environmental scanning can help us understand how the company has anticipated and responded to the external trends that have shaped its terrain.

Political: Tesla has navigated political challenges, such as regulatory barriers, government subsidies, and trade disputes, by advocating for policies that promote electric vehicles and renewable energy.

Economic: Tesla has capitalized on economic trends, such as the rise of the sharing economy and the increasing demand for sustainable products and services by launching innovative business models such as Tesla Energy and Tesla Network.

Sociocultural: Tesla has aligned with sociocultural trends, such as the growing awareness of climate change and the desire for eco-friendly products, by emphasizing its mission to accelerate the world's transition to sustainable energy and by designing sleek and futuristic electric vehicles that appeal to environmentally conscious consumers.

Technological: Tesla has leveraged technological advancements, such as battery storage, autonomous driving, and artificial intelligence, by investing heavily in research and development and by constantly improving its products and services to stay ahead of the competition.

Legal: Tesla has responded to legal challenges, such as intellectual property disputes and labor issues, by hiring top lawyers and lobbyists and by advocating for policies that promote innovation and fairness in the marketplace

Environmental: Tesla has embraced environmental sustainability as a core value and has developed products and services that enable individuals and organizations to reduce their carbon footprint and contribute to a cleaner and healthier planet.

Conclusion

In today's rapidly changing business environment, it is more important than ever for businesses to conduct environmental scanning and use tools like PESTLE analysis to map their business terrain. By identifying key external factors and developing strategies to address them, businesses can remain competitive and stay ahead of the curve. While external factors may be beyond the control of the organization, by staying informed and regularly updating business strategies, businesses can mitigate risk and take advantage of opportunities presented by the external environment. By conducting thorough PESTLE analyses and remaining vigilant, we can chart our course with confidence and make strategic decisions that propel us toward success.

Chapter 10

Developing Your Strategy: SWOT Matrix

After completing your SWOT analysis and environmental scanning, it's time to craft a top-notch strategy. Think of it as a high-stakes game of chess, where you must leverage your strengths, tackle your weaknesses, and seize every opportunity that comes your way. And the SWOT matrix? Consider it your trusty playbook. In this chapter, we'll delve into two key frameworks that will help you develop a winning strategy and achieve your desired outcomes. Get ready to take the business world by storm!

SWOT Matrix

The SWOT matrix is a powerful tool that takes the insights from your SWOT analysis and transforms them into a strategic plan. It maps the internal strengths and weaknesses of your organization against the external opportunities and threats, creating four strategic quadrants: Strengths-Opportunities (SO), Strengths-Threats (ST), Weaknesses-Opportunities (WO), and

Weaknesses-Threats (WT). Each quadrant represents a different strategy that can help you achieve your desired outcomes.

SO Strategy: Leveraging Strengths to Seize Opportunities

The SO Strategy is where you unleash the full power of your strengths to seize the golden opportunities that lie before you. Picture this: you have an incredible strength, let's say it's your expertise in a particular field. Now imagine that there's a fantastic opportunity in that field, a growing demand that you can capitalize on. With the SO strategy, you develop a plan to expand your services and offerings, meet that demand head-on, and make a splash in the market

ST Strategy: Turning Strengths into Shields Against Threats

In the game of business, there will be plenty of threats to mitigate. But with the ST strategy, you can transform your strengths into impenetrable shields that protect you from those threats. Imagine that your powerful strength is your established brand and reputation. Now, in the distance, you see a new competitor emerging, threatening to steal your thunder. But with the ST strategy, you develop a plan to strengthen your brand, differentiate your offerings, and maintain your competitive edge. You become a conqueror.

WO Strategy: Addressing Weaknesses to Seize Opportunities

Weaknesses are like hidden treasures waiting to be discovered. The WO strategy enables you uncover weaknesses and transform them into steppingstones to success. Perhaps your weakness is your lack of a strong online presence. But wait, there's an opportunity on the horizon, a growing demand for e-commerce. With the WO strategy, you develop a plan to invest in digital marketing, embrace e-commerce platforms, and reach more customers than ever before. You can turn your weakness into a victory!

WT Strategy: Addressing Weaknesses to Mitigate Threats

In the game of business, threats are like stormy seas that can sink your ship. But with the WT strategy, you can navigate those treacherous waters and keep your ship afloat. Let's say your weakness is your limited resources. And on the horizon, you spot a threat, an intensifying competition. But with the WT strategy, you develop a plan to streamline your operations, optimize your resources, reduce costs, and increase efficiency. It's like building a sturdy ship that can weather any storm!

Case Study: Amazon SWOT Matrix

Now, let's take a closer look at the e-commerce giant, Amazon, and examine how they've utilized the SWOT matrix to chart their course to success.

Strengths:

- *Diverse product range:* Amazon offers a wide range of products and services, including books, electronics, apparel, music and video streaming, cloud computing services, and much more. This allows the company to appeal to a broad customer base and generate significant revenue streams.
- *Leading online retailer:* Amazon is the world's largest online retailer, with a significant market share in many countries. This gives the company a competitive advantage over other retailers in terms of brand recognition, customer trust, and economies of scale.

- *Strong brand reputation:* Amazon has a strong brand reputation, built on its commitment to customer service, innovation, and convenience. This reputation helps to attract and retain customers, as well as to recruit and retain top talent.
- *Innovation:* Amazon has a culture of innovation, which has led to the development of new products and services, such as Amazon Web Services (AWS), Amazon Prime, and Alexa. This allows the company to stay ahead of competitors and to expand into new markets.

Weaknesses:
- *Dependence on third-party sellers:* A significant portion of Amazon's revenue comes from third-party sellers on its platform. This dependence can create risks such as counterfeit products and product quality issues, which can damage the company's reputation.
- *Negative public perception:* Amazon has faced criticism over issues such as worker conditions and environmental impact. This negative public perception can harm the company's reputation and lead to decreased customer loyalty and sales.
- *Limited physical presence:* While Amazon has expanded its physical presence through acquisitions such as Whole Foods and the launch of Amazon Go stores, the company still has limited physical retail presence compared to competitors. This can limit the

company's ability to reach customers who prefer to shop in-store.

- *High competition:* Amazon faces intense competition from other retailers and e-commerce companies, such as Walmart, Alibaba, and eBay. This can limit the company's market share and profitability.

Opportunities:

- *Expanding product range:* Amazon can continue to expand its product range, by adding new categories or developing its own private label products. This can attract new customers and increase revenue streams.
- *Global expansion:* Amazon can expand its operations into new markets, such as Asia and Africa, to tap into new customer segments and increase its market share.
- *Growth of cloud computing:* AWS is a significant source of revenue for Amazon, and the growth of cloud computing is expected to continue. Amazon can continue to invest in this area to maintain its leadership position and expand its offerings.
- *Innovation:* Amazon can continue to innovate in areas such as artificial intelligence, machine learning, and voice-activated technologies, to develop new products and services that meet evolving customer needs.

Threats:

- *Regulation:* Amazon faces the risk of increased regulation, particularly around antitrust concerns and worker conditions. This can lead to increased costs and restrictions on the company's operations.

- *Cybersecurity risks:* As a large and highly visible company, Amazon is a target for cyber attacks. These attacks can lead to data breaches, which can damage the company's reputation and lead to legal liabilities.
- *Economic conditions:* Economic downturns can lead to decreased consumer spending, which can impact Amazon's revenue and profitability.
- *Intense competition:* Amazon faces intense competition from a variety of competitors, including traditional retailers, e-commerce companies, and technology companies. This can limit the company's market share and profitability.

Conclusion

The SWOT matrix is a powerful tool that guides organizations like Amazon in developing a strategic plan that aligns with their goals, strengths, and opportunities while mitigating weaknesses and threats. By analyzing Amazon's SWOT matrix, we can see that their strengths, such as their diverse product range, leading online retailer status, strong brand reputation, and culture of innovation, provide significant opportunities for growth. However, they must also address weaknesses like dependence on third-party sellers, negative public perception, limited physical presence, and intense competition. To mitigate threats, they need to navigate potential regulation, cybersecurity risks, economic conditions, and intense competition. The SWOT matrix acts as their compass, guiding them through uncharted territories to achieve their desired outcomes.

So, my fellow strategists, embrace the power of the SWOT matrix, let it be your trusted companion on the journey to success. Leverage your strengths, shore up your weaknesses, seize every opportunity, and navigate the stormy seas of threats. With the SWOT matrix as your guide, you'll be equipped to conquer the business world and emerge victorious.

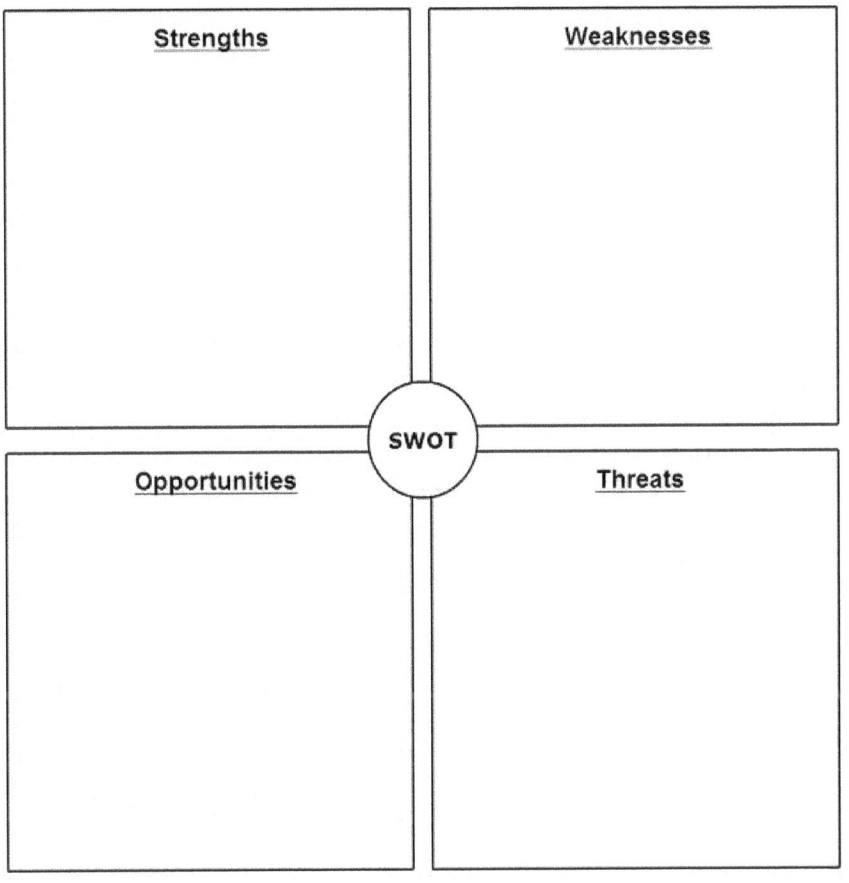

In today's constantly evolving business environment, understanding the competitive forces at play in an industry is more critical than ever.

Chapter 11

Developing Your Strategy: Porter's Five Forces

Porter's Five Forces, the trusty sword of the discerning business strategist! This formidable framework, forged by the wise Michael E. Porter of Harvard Business School fame, has been honed to perfection since the late 1970s. Porter's Five Forces is a powerful tool in the arsenal of any savvy business strategist. This framework has been refined over decades to provide a comprehensive analysis of the competitive forces within an industry. It is used by managers and analysts worldwide to assess the attractiveness of an industry and identify key drivers of profitability. So let's roll up our sleeves and dive into the world of strategic analysis with the assistance of Porter's Five Forces, a framework for analyzing the competitive forces in any industry.

The five forces that Porter identified are:
1. Threat of new entrants
2. Bargaining power of suppliers
3. Bargaining power of buyers
4. Threat of substitutes

5. Rivalry among existing competitors

Each of these forces represents a different aspect of the competitive landscape of an industry. By analyzing these forces, businesses can gain insights into the structure and dynamics of their industry and identify the key drivers of profitability. Let's take a look at each of these in more detail.

Threat of new entrants

The threat of new entrants represents the degree to which new competitors can enter an industry and compete with existing businesses. Factors that can increase the threat of new entrants include low barriers to entry, such as low startup costs, and a lack of established brand loyalty among consumers. Other factors that can increase the threat of new entrants include the availability of substitute products and the ease of access to distribution channels.

Bargaining power of suppliers

The bargaining power of suppliers represents the degree to which suppliers can influence the price and quality of the goods and services they provide to businesses. Factors that can increase the bargaining power of suppliers include a small number of suppliers in the industry, high switching costs for businesses, and the presence of unique or specialized inputs that are difficult to replace.

Bargaining power of buyers

The bargaining power of buyers represents the degree to which buyers can influence the price and quality of the goods and services they purchase from businesses. Factors that can increase the bargaining power of buyers include a large number of buyers in the industry, low switching costs for buyers, and the presence of substitute products that give buyers more options.

Threat of substitutes

The threat of substitutes represents the degree to which substitute products can compete with existing products in an industry. Factors that can increase the threat of substitutes include the availability of substitute products that are cheaper or more convenient than existing products, and the willingness of consumers to switch to substitute products.

Rivalry among existing competitors

Rivalry among existing competitors represents the degree of competition between businesses in an industry. Factors that can increase rivalry among competitors include a large number of competitors in the industry, slow industry growth, high fixed costs, and high exit barriers.

Porter's Five Forces can be used to assess the attractiveness of an industry and to identify the key drivers of profitability. By analyzing each of the five forces, businesses can gain insights into the competitive landscape of their industry and identify areas of opportunity and risk. For example, if the threat of new entrants is low and the bargaining power of suppliers is high, businesses may need to focus on building strong relationships with their suppliers to ensure that they have access to the inputs they need at a reasonable price.

Similarly, if the threat of substitutes is high, businesses may need to focus on differentiating their products or services to make them more attractive to consumers. By using Porter's Five Forces to assess their industry, businesses can develop strategies to improve their competitive position and achieve long-term profitability.

Case Study: Apple Using Porter's Five Forces

Apple is a multinational technology company that designs, develops, and sells consumer electronics, computer software, and online services. Apple's success can be attributed to its ability to leverage Porter's Five Forces to gain and maintain a competitive advantage.

1. *Threat of New Entrants:* The threat of new entrants in the technology industry is relatively low due to high barriers to entry, such as intellectual property rights, economies of scale, and capital requirements. Apple has established a strong brand and reputation and has invested heavily in research and development to stay ahead of emerging technologies.
2. *Bargaining Power of Suppliers:* The bargaining power of suppliers in the technology industry is moderate to high due to the concentration of suppliers and their ability to dictate terms and prices. Apple has built strong relationships with its suppliers and has invested in vertical integration to reduce its reliance on external suppliers.
3. *Bargaining Power of Buyers:* The bargaining power of buyers in the technology industry is high due to the availability of alternative products and the ease of switching. Apple has developed a loyal customer base through its unique design, user experience, and ecosystem of products and services.
4. *Threat of Substitute Products or Services:* The threat of substitute products or services in the technology industry is moderate to high due to the availability of alternative products and services. Apple has differentiated its products and services through design, innovation, and quality and has developed a

strong ecosystem of products and services to increase customer loyalty and retention.
5. *Rivalry Among Existing Competitors:* The rivalry among existing competitors in the technology industry is intense due to the large number of players and the high stakes involved. Apple has differentiated itself through its design, innovation, and quality and has developed a strong ecosystem of products and services to increase customer loyalty and retention.

Conclusion

Porter's Five Forces framework is a powerful tool for analyzing the competitive dynamics of an industry. By examining the five forces of competition, businesses can gain a better understanding of the key drivers of profitability and identify areas of opportunity and risk. This framework has become a standard tool in business strategy and is widely used by managers and analysts to assess the attractiveness of an industry.

The five forces of competition, which include the threat of new entrants, bargaining power of suppliers, bargaining power of buyers, threat of substitutes, and rivalry among existing competitors, represent different aspects of the competitive landscape of an industry. Each force can significantly impact a business's profitability and success.

For businesses facing a high threat of new entrants, they may need to focus on building strong relationships with suppliers to ensure access to the inputs they need at a reasonable price. Similarly, if the threat of substitutes is high, businesses may need to focus on differentiating their products or services to make them more appealing to consumers.

By using Porter's Five Forces framework to assess their industry, businesses can develop strategies to improve their competitive position and achieve long-term profitability. This framework provides businesses with valuable insights into the structure and dynamics of their industry, allowing them to identify areas where they can gain a competitive advantage.

In today's constantly evolving business environment, understanding the competitive forces at play in an industry is more critical than ever. Porter's Five Forces framework remains a valuable tool for businesses seeking to gain a

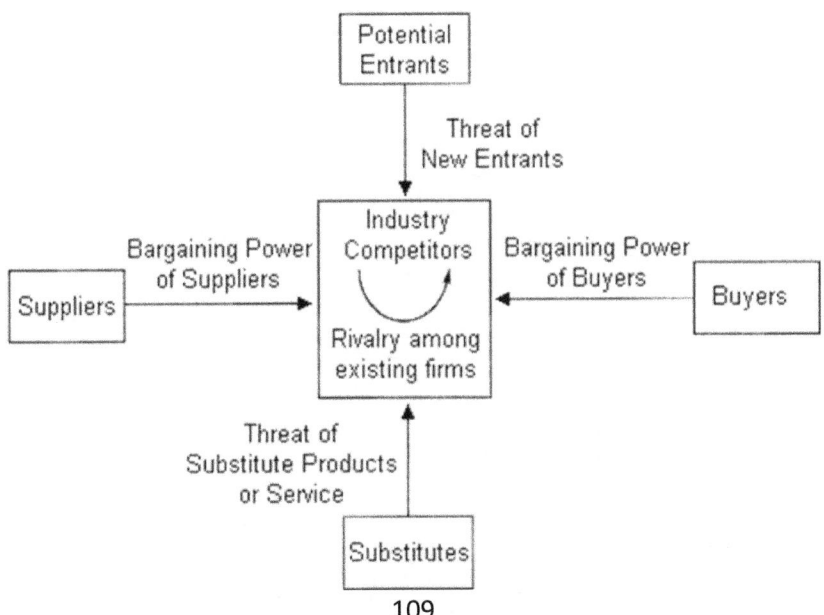

competitive edge, improve their profitability, and achieve long-term success.

Chapter 12

Creating Your Action Plan: To-Do Lists and Milestones

Ah, the art of goal-setting and strategy development—a fine pursuit for any self-respecting business aficionado. But let us not forget the crucial ingredient that separates the champions from the also-rans: action! Without a well-crafted action plan in place, your goals and strategies will remain mere fantasies, lost in the ether of unfulfilled potential.

But here's your solution: the formidable action plan. This mighty roadmap will guide you through the treacherous terrain of execution, providing a clear and organized path to your desired outcomes. In this chapter, we will explore a range of tools and techniques that will equip you with the skills to create a truly effective action plan, including the trusty to-do list and the ever-reliable milestone. So let's take a look:

To-Do Lists

To-do lists are a valuable and practical tool that can greatly enhance your ability to manage daily tasks and activities. By utilizing to-do lists effectively, you can prioritize your tasks, maintain organization, and combat procrastination. If you've ever hosted a holiday gathering, you'll understand the importance of this!

Here are some key benefits of incorporating to-do lists into your routine:

- *Enhanced Focus:* When you create a to-do list, it enables you to concentrate your attention on the most crucial tasks and avoid being sidetracked by distractions.
- *Increased Productivity:* To-do lists excel at boosting productivity by breaking down larger, more intimidating tasks into smaller, more manageable ones. This approach helps you maintain a steady workflow and progress toward your goals.
- *Stress Reduction:* To-do lists have the power to alleviate stress by providing a sense of control and accomplishment as you cross off completed tasks. They serve as a visual representation of your progress and give you a clear picture of what remains to be done.

To create an effective to-do list, consider the following tips:

- *Prioritize Tasks:* Identify the tasks that hold the highest importance and place them at the top of your list. This way, you can address critical responsibilities first and prevent them from being overshadowed by less significant ones. Sometimes your to-do list can act as a "brain dump," getting all your swirling thoughts down onto a list so that your mind can focus on what matters at the moment.

- *Break Down Larger Tasks:* Tackle overwhelming tasks by breaking them down into smaller, more manageable subtasks. This strategy promotes a sense of achievement as you complete each subtask, and it propels you forward.
- *Set Deadlines:* Assign deadlines to each task on your to-do list. Having time limits encourages you to stay on track and fosters a sense of urgency, aiding in efficient task completion.
- *Regularly Review and Update:* Make it a habit to review and update your to-do list on a regular basis. This practice ensures that you remain focused on your priorities and can make adjustments as new tasks arise or circumstances change.

By embracing the power of to-do lists and implementing these recommendations, you can supercharge your productivity, minimize stress, and achieve a greater sense of control over your daily responsibilities.

Gantt Charts

Gantt charts are powerful visual tools used in project management to plan, schedule, and track progress. Named after their creator Henry Gantt, an American mechanical engineer and management consultant, these charts provide a clear overview of project tasks, timelines, and dependencies.

By organizing project activities in a horizontal bar chart format, Gantt charts offer a simplified way to manage complex projects and communicate project plans effectively.

The main components of a Gantt chart include tasks, timelines, and dependencies. Each task is represented by a horizontal bar that spans the duration of the task. The length of the bar indicates the estimated or actual time required to complete the task. The chart's vertical axis lists the tasks, while the horizontal axis represents the project timeline, usually measured in days, weeks, or months.

Dependencies between tasks are illustrated by linking bars. These connections indicate that a specific task must be completed before another task can begin. By visualizing task dependencies, Gantt charts help project managers identify critical path activities and potential bottlenecks that can impact project schedules.

Gantt charts offer numerous benefits. Firstly, they provide a clear and concise overview of the project, making it easy to understand the project's scope, timeline, and progress at a glance. This visual representation facilitates effective communication among project team members, stakeholders, and clients. It ensures that everyone has a shared understanding of the project's goals and deadlines.

Moreover, Gantt charts aid in project planning by allowing managers to allocate resources efficiently. By visualizing task durations and dependencies, project managers can assign resources effectively, ensuring that each task has the necessary personnel and equipment to be completed on time. This helps optimize resource utilization and prevents bottlenecks caused by resource constraints.

Another advantage of Gantt charts is that they support project tracking and progress monitoring. As tasks are completed, the corresponding bars on the chart are shaded or marked as complete. This visual representation enables project managers to track the project's actual progress against the planned schedule. Deviations from the original plan can be easily identified, allowing managers to take corrective actions promptly and adjust the project timeline if necessary.

Gantt charts also foster collaboration and coordination among team members. By providing a shared visualization of project tasks and deadlines, team members can understand their roles, responsibilities, and how their work contributes to the overall project. This promotes better coordination and collaboration, ensuring that everyone is aligned towards achieving project milestones.

In addition, Gantt charts facilitate project reporting and documentation. The visual representation of project plans and progress can be easily exported and shared in reports or presentations. This simplifies the process of reporting project status to stakeholders and clients, as the information is presented in a clear and structured manner.

However, Gantt charts also have limitations. They can become complex and overwhelming for large-scale projects with numerous interdependencies. In such cases, the chart may become cluttered, making it difficult to comprehend the overall project structure. Additionally, Gantt charts are static representations and may not capture real-time changes or unexpected events that occur during project execution.

To overcome these limitations, modern project management tools often incorporate interactive Gantt charts that can be updated in real-time, allowing project managers to adapt plans dynamically as circumstances change. These tools also offer features like task dependencies, resource allocation, and progress tracking, making project management more efficient and collaborative.

Gantt charts are valuable tools for project managers to plan, schedule, and track projects effectively. They continue to be widely used and are often integrated into project management software to enhance their functionality and usability. Just be sure that if you use them, they are clear and concise and don't overwhelm the project.

Milestones

If you've ever had a "milestone birthday," then you understand the significance of the word. Milestones are important events or achievements that mark progress toward your goals in both life and business. They can measure your journey, celebrate your successes, and motivate you to keep going. Milestones can help you:

- *Measure progress:* By setting milestones, you can measure your progress towards your goals and make adjustments as needed. Set deadlines for each milestone to help you stay on track. Most writers are great at doing this. Some outline their entire book chapter by chapter before they begin to write. Others simply set a word count milestone each day.

- *Celebrate achievements:* Milestones provide an opportunity to celebrate your achievements and motivate you to keep going. When you finish that chapter or reach that word count, treat yourself to a trip to the bookstore or buy yourself a special bookmark.

- *Stay motivated:* By breaking down your goals into smaller, more achievable milestones, you can stay motivated and focused on your progress. Again, the chapter-by-chapter deadline works well here. Or, if you are tracking sales, perhaps start with one small sale per day/week/month (depending on your product.) Or maybe just having a positive conversation with a potential new client can be your goal for that day.

Case Study: Airbnb

Founded in 2008 by Brian Chesky, Joe Gebbia, and Nathan Blecharczyk, Airbnb is a platform that connects travelers with hosts who offer unique and affordable accommodations around the world. The company was started to solve a problem the founders encountered while living in San Francisco: they couldn't afford their rent, so they decided to rent out their living room to attendees of a design conference. This experience led them to launch Airbnb, which has since grown into a global brand with over 4 million listings in 220 countries and regions.

One of the keys to Airbnb's success has been its ability to execute on its strategies through careful planning and action. The company has used tools like Gantt charts, to-do lists, and milestones to create a clear and organized plan for achieving its goals. For example, when Airbnb decided to expand globally, the company created a detailed action plan that included breaking down the process into smaller, more manageable steps, setting deadlines, and tracking progress along the way. This allowed Airbnb to successfully expand into new markets and establish itself as a global brand.

Another example of Airbnb's effective use of action planning can be seen in the company's response to the COVID-19 pandemic. In 2020, when the pandemic hit and the travel industry came to a standstill, Airbnb was faced with a significant challenge. However, the company quickly pivoted its strategy and created a new action plan that included launching online experiences, expanding its cleaning protocols, and partnering with local governments to offer temporary housing for frontline workers. By executing this plan, Airbnb was able to weather the storm of the pandemic and emerge as a stronger company.

Overall, Airbnb's success can be attributed in part to its careful planning and execution of strategies through the use of tools like Gantt charts, to-do lists, and milestones. By breaking down larger goals into smaller, more achievable tasks and tracking progress along the way, Airbnb has been able to achieve its desired outcomes and establish itself as a leader in the travel industry.

Conclusion

Creating an action plan is crucial to achieving your desired outcomes, whether it's launching a business, achieving a personal goal, or completing a project. By using tools like Gantt charts, to-do lists, and milestones, you can create a clear and organized plan to execute your strategies effectively. These tools can help you stay focused, improve productivity, and measure progress toward your goals. Remember to break down larger goals into smaller, more achievable tasks, set deadlines, and celebrate each milestone achievement to stay motivated and on track.

Chapter 13

Building Your Support Network: Mentors, Allies, and Accountability Partners

When it comes to staying motivated and on track towards your goals, a support network is essential. This group of individuals provides the much-needed guidance, encouragement, and accountability to keep you focused and driven. In this chapter, we'll explore the different types of support networks that exist, from the wise and experienced mentor to the loyal and dependable ally, and the ever-vigilant accountability partner. Let's take a look.

Mentors

A mentor is an experienced and knowledgeable individual who can provide guidance and advice based on their own experiences. Mentors can help you:

- *Gain new insights and perspectives.* Mentors can share their own experiences and knowledge to help you learn from them, the seasoned veterans they are. Think of the old days when it was more customary to have apprentices. Young men and women worked under a professional to learn the trade, kind of like a mentor, in industries like tannery, blacksmithing, and carpentry. These older individuals knew the little tips and tricks to made the work easier, and they knew the best products to use. Does a certain hide tan easier than another? Do you create different types of shoes for horses who do different tasks? Since they had already "been there, done that", these skilled professionals had great knowledge to share with their apprentices, so these younger folks could already have a head start. We don't need to go back to the olden days to experience this. Today, mentors can give insights into skilled trades, business growth, entrepreneurship, finance . . . the list goes on. Why learn something from the beginning when you can find a mentor who will share the ropes with you?

- *Avoid common mistakes.* Mentors can help you avoid common errors and pitfalls by sharing their own lessons learned. They have figured out what works better, and what not to do.
- *Build your network.* Just like the blacksmiths probably had a customer base that the apprentice could start working with, mentors today can introduce you to new contacts and expand your professional reach. These individuals probably already know quite a few people in the field. Networking is a great way to build your support.

To find a mentor, look for individuals who have experience in your field or have achieved similar goals to yours. You can also reach out to professional associations or use online mentorship platforms such as LinkedIn. Rotary Clubs, business organizations in your town and the Chamber of Commerce are great places to start. Also, many community colleges have clubs or groups such as the Economics Club and the Pipefitters Association, etc. where you can meet people in your field.

Allies

Allies are individuals who share your values and goals and can provide support and encouragement as you work towards your desired outcomes. Allies can help you:

- *Stay motivated.* Allies can provide encouragement and support to get you through even when things get tough.
- *Provide feedback.* Allies can provide commentary and constructive criticism to help you improve and make progress.
- *Share resources.* Allies can share their own resources, knowledge, and contacts to help you achieve your goals.

One great example of allies coming together is a group of authors. In a good writer's group, there isn't the threat of competition, even though everyone wants to get published. Instead, writers encourage each other to meet their writing goals, be it a page count or a word count. At meetings, they read and critique each other's work, providing feedback on character strengths, dialogue, or chapter length. They also often share resources, like how to reach your target audience, or which artists design the best book covers at the most reasonable price.

To find allies, look for individuals with similar values and goals as yours. You can join online communities, attend events or conferences, or connect with like-minded individuals on social media.

Accountability Partners

An accountability partner is someone who holds you accountable for your actions and commitments. They provide a level of external accountability that can help you stay on track and achieve your goals. Accountability partners can help you:

- *Stay focused.* Accountability partners can help you stay focused on your goals by reminding you of your commitments. They should have a regular check-in time with you daily or weekly, to see if you are on track.
- *Avoid procrastination.* Accountability partners can help you avoid procrastination and stay productive by holding you accountable for your actions. They can provide encouragement and remind you of why you created the goals in the first place.

- *Celebrate successes.* Accountability partners can celebrate your successes with you, providing motivation to keep going. Go out and share a meal or a coffee, or go see that game you've been wanting to see.

To find an accountability partner, look for someone you trust and respect who has similar goals and values as yours. You can also use online accountability platforms.

Case Study: Facebook's Sheryl Sandberg

Sheryl Sandberg is the COO of Facebook and author of the book *Lean In*. Sandberg is known for her advocacy of mentorship and support networks for women in the workplace. She has spoken openly about the role of her mentors, including Larry Summers and Mark Zuckerberg, in her career success and has also founded the non-profit organization Lean In, which aims to empower women to achieve their professional goals through mentorship and support networks. Additionally, Sandberg created Lean In Circles "because there's so much power when women come together to help each other," Sandburg says. These Circles are made up of small groups of women who meet to give and get advice, celebrate each other's wins, and to help each other achieve their goals.

"I wanted to create a place where women—in every industry and at any stage of their careers—could find connection and be encouraged to go after their dreams. Circles took off in ways I could never have imagined. Now more than 75,000 women have created Lean In Circles in 181 countries," she says.

Sandberg's example illustrates the importance of seeking out mentors and allies to help navigate the challenges and opportunities of professional life and the power of building a supportive community to achieve one's goals.

Conclusion

Building a support network is an essential part of achieving your desired outcomes. By having mentors, allies, and accountability partners, you can gain new insights, stay motivated, avoid common mistakes, and hold yourself accountable for your actions. Remember, your support network can be a valuable resource as you work towards your goals, so don't be afraid to reach out and build connections.

With time, money, and energy all vying for our attention, it's no wonder we sometimes feel like we're juggling chainsaws while riding a unicycle.

Chapter 14

Managing Your Resources: Time, Money, and Energy

Ah, managing resources—the ultimate balancing act for the modern-day business juggler. With time, money, and energy all vying for our attention, it's no wonder we sometimes feel like we're juggling chainsaws while riding a unicycle. In this chapter we'll explore the art of resource management and how to use your limited assets to achieve your desired outcomes without losing your sanity (or your fingers). So let's sharpen those management skills and get ready to juggle those resources like a Fortune 500 executive.

Time Management

Time is a limited resource, and it is essential to manage it effectively to achieve your goals. Time management involves planning and organizing your time to maximize productivity and achieve your desired outcomes. Here are some tips for effective time management:
- *Set Priorities:* Identify your most important tasks and prioritize them based on their importance and urgency. Often, doing the hardest thing first gets it out

of the way and then motivates you to do the easier tasks.

- *Create a Schedule:* Develop a schedule that allows you to allocate your time effectively between your various tasks and activities. You can use a paper planner or an online tool. Write (or type) down everything you need to do and figure out how much time to allocate to each task. Once you have everything in front of you, it's easier to navigate.

- *Eliminate Distractions:* Minimize distractions and interruptions by turning off notifications, closing unnecessary tabs, and focusing on one task at a time. Also, research has also shown that doing things in batches, instead of small, incremental tasks, is more productive. For example, take a block of time, like an hour, and read all of your emails, instead of reading them as they come in, disrupting your flow of thought on something else.

- *Avoid Procrastination:* Break tasks down into smaller, manageable tasks and tackle them one at a time to avoid procrastination.

- *Delegate Tasks:* Delegate tasks to others where possible to free up time for more critical tasks.

- *Track Your Time:* Use time tracking tools to monitor how you spend your time and make adjustments as necessary.

Money Management

Money is another critical resource, and it is essential to manage it effectively to achieve your goals. Money management involves creating a budget, tracking your expenses, and making informed decisions about your spending. Here are some tips for effective money management:

- *Create a Budget:* Develop a budget that outlines your income and expenses and allocate your money accordingly.

- *Track Your Expenses:* Keep track of your expenses to ensure you stay within your budget and identify areas where you can reduce spending. Be very consistent about jotting down expenses. I have a friend who puts all of her receipts into a box, and then takes every Friday morning to track the expenses in her software.

- *Save for the Future:* Set aside money for future goals, emergencies, and retirement to ensure you are financially secure. It will give you peace of mind, and if an emergency comes up, such as a large repair, you won't have to scramble to figure out where the funds will come from.

- *Make Informed Decisions:* Make informed decisions about your spending by weighing the costs and benefits and considering your long-term financial goals. One rule of thumb is to not buy anything on a whim. Wait at least 24 hours and if you still want it, then look at your budget and see if you can fit it in.

Energy Management

Energy is a crucial resource that is often overlooked. Managing your energy involves taking care of your physical and mental health to maintain high levels of energy and focus. Here are some tips for effective energy management:

- *Take Breaks:* Take regular breaks to avoid burnout and maintain productivity. If you have a desk job, set a timer to get up and stretch, and rest your eyes from the computer. If you have a physical job, make sure you take breaks to rest.
- *Get Enough Sleep:* Get enough sleep to ensure you have the energy to tackle your tasks and activities. Do what you have to do to make your bedroom comfortable. Use white noise, room-darkening drapes, and essential oils if they help. Avoid screentime or anything with a blue light at least an hour before bed.
- *Exercise Regularly:* Exercise regularly to improve your physical and mental health and increase your energy levels. It's hard to fit in, I know, but make it a priority and when you are filling out your planner, make sure it's in there. It should be as important as anything else you do. Don't fall into the trap of, "I don't have enough time." *Make* the time. You can't take care of everything else if your body is failing you.
- *Eat Healthy:* Eat a balanced diet to fuel your body and mind and maintain high levels of energy. This might

take some advanced meal planning so you're not scrambling at the last minute. Take a few hours one day a week to plan and prepare. There are great ideas on social media about how to make freezer meals ahead of time, or how to pre-chop veggies and meat for several nights' dinners. I hear Instagram and Pinterest are perfect for that . . .not that I personally spend much time there . . .

- *Practice Mindfulness:* Practice mindfulness and meditation to reduce stress and increase focus and productivity. One good habit is to take fifteen minutes in the morning to say gratitudes or journal, and then just sit quietly focusing on your breathing. Do the focused breathing again at the end of your workday, or before bed, to give your mind a chance to relax and quiet down.

Time is a limited resource, and it is essential to manage it effectively to achieve your goals.

Case Study: Elizabeth Holmes, Founder of Theranos

Elizabeth Holmes, the founder of Theranos, a blood testing company, is a prime example of the importance of managing your resources effectively. In 2015, Holmes was worth an estimated $4.5 billion and was hailed as the youngest female self-made billionaire in history. However, by 2018, her net worth had plummeted to zero, and she was facing criminal charges for fraud.

One of the reasons for Holmes' downfall was her mismanagement of resources, particularly her company's finances. She spent lavishly on her lifestyle, including private jets, luxurious homes, and expensive cars. She also spent heavily on advertising and marketing campaigns, even though her company's product was not yet proven to work.

Holmes also mismanaged her company's time and energy. She pushed her employees to work long hours and prioritize their work over their health and well-being. She also created a culture of fear and intimidation, where employees were afraid to speak out about the company's problems.

The lessons we can learn from Elizabeth Holmes' story are clear: effective resource management is essential for achieving success. By prioritizing our time, money, and energy, we can make progress toward our goals and avoid the pitfalls that led to Holmes' downfall.

Conclusion

Managing your resources effectively is essential for achieving your desired outcomes, whether they are personal or professional. By prioritizing your time, money, and energy, you can make progress toward your goals and avoid the pitfalls that can lead to failure. Use the tips and real-life examples provided in this chapter to take control of your resources and maximize your chances of success.

In a constantly evolving world, cultivating your skills and knowledge is vital.

Chapter 15

Cultivating Your Skills and Knowledge: Learning Plans and Self-Development

In today's rapidly changing world, the age-old question remains of how to stay relevant in a world that changes faster than a Kardashian's wardrobe. In this chapter, we'll delve into the art of self-development and creating a learning plan that will make you feel like the Einstein of Wall Street. From reading books to attending seminars to binge-watching TED Talks, we'll explore a range of strategies to help you stay ahead of the game and achieve your goals. So let's get ready to sharpen those brain cells and become the ultimate learning machine!

Why Cultivating Your Skills and Knowledge Is Important

The world is constantly evolving, and technology is advancing at an unprecedented pace. The skills and knowledge that were once sufficient are no longer enough to keep up with the demands of the modern world. Cultivating your skills and knowledge is vital for the following reasons:

- *Increased Productivity:* When you acquire new skills and knowledge, you become more efficient and productive.
- *Career Advancement:* Continual learning helps you stay relevant in your industry and can lead to career advancement.
- *Personal Growth:* Learning and self-development can help you grow as a person and lead a more fulfilling life.

Creating a Learning Plan

To cultivate your skills and knowledge effectively, you need a plan. Here are some steps to help you create a learning plan:

- *Set Goals:* Identify your long-term and short-term goals and determine the skills and knowledge you need to achieve them. What do you want to learn? How far do you want to reach? Do you want to be an efficient salesperson, or do you want to be the *best* salesperson in the state? Do you want to make the swim team, or are you vying for the Olympics?
- *Identify Resources:* Identify the resources available to you, such as books, courses, mentors, and experts in your field.
- *Create a Schedule:* Develop a schedule that allows you to allocate time for learning and development. If

it seems overwhelming, break it down into small segments.
- *Track Your Progress:* Monitor your progress regularly to ensure you are on track to achieving your goals.

Self-Development Strategies

Brene Brown, an American professor, social worker and bestselling author, reminds us that self-love comes before success, not the other way around.

"If you don't strive to be the best version of yourself, you're leaving a lot of life on the table," says Brown. "You won't develop your talents. You won't examine your beliefs. You won't work to improve yourself. On the other hand, if you're <u>always hunting the next win</u> and pushing yourself to be better, you're not going to enjoy the present or like yourself very much along the way. That's no way to go through life."

So there must be a balance. While we're out there striving to be successful, to be entrepreneurs, or to reach our goals and desired outcomes, we must also, and first, make ourselves into something we love. We must nurture and care for ourselves, much like you would a child or someone else you love.

It's not selfish to work on yourself. I mean, it *can* be, if that's all we think of is "me me me." But done well, the more you improve yourself, the more you have to offer others. Self improvement will boost your confidence and help improve your relationships.

Here are some strategies you can use to cultivate your skills and knowledge:

- *Read Widely:* Read books, articles, and blogs on a variety of topics to expand your knowledge.
- *Attend Conferences and Seminars:* Industry conferences and seminars are a great place to learn from experts and offer you the opportunity to network with other professionals.
- *Take Online Courses:* Online courses are a convenient way to learn new skills and knowledge on your schedule.
- *Seek Feedback:* Ask for feedback from peers, mentors, and experts to identify areas where you can improve.
- *Practice Regularly:* Regular practice is essential for mastering skills and retaining knowledge. In his bestselling book *Outliers: The Story of Success,* Malcolm Gladwell says, "the key to achieving true expertise in any skill is simply a matter of practicing, albeit in the correct way, for at least 10 000 hours." Yeah, we don't all have 10,000 hours to devote to the violin or our golf swing, but you get the point.

- *Work with a Mentor:* Working with a mentor can provide you with valuable insights and guidance on your journey to self-development.
- *Network:* Networking with other professionals in your field can help you learn about new opportunities and stay up to date on industry trends.

Case Study: Kobe Bryant

Kobe Bryant, the late NBA superstar, is an excellent example of the importance of self-development and continual learning. Throughout his career, Bryant was known for his relentless work ethic and dedication to self-improvement. He was known to get up as early as 3 a.m. to practice and could often be seen practicing before and after the actual scheduled practices. He continually worked on his skills and knowledge, even when he was already considered one of the best players in the league. He ate, slept, and dreamed his game.

Bryant's dedication to self-improvement paid off, as he won five NBA championships, two Olympic gold medals, and numerous individual awards throughout his career. He also established a successful business career after retiring from basketball.

Bryant's approach to self-development involved setting clear goals, identifying areas where he needed to improve, and working tirelessly to achieve his objectives. He was also known for seeking out mentors and experts in his field to learn from their experiences and knowledge.

The lessons we can learn from Kobe Bryant's story are clear: to achieve success, we must continually work on our skills and knowledge, set clear goals, and seek out mentors and experts to learn from their experiences.

But be careful. Remember to take care of yourself and not burn out. It's all about balance. Even Bryant needed to rest.

Tim Grover, his personal trainer and mental coach, made sure the NBA champion took breaks to avoid burnout. He taught him how to set realistic expectations for himself, how to say no to others, and to take some time for himself. He helped Bryant learn how to work smarter, not just harder.

Conclusion

Cultivating your skills and knowledge is essential for achieving success and realizing your desired outcomes. Creating a learning plan and following self-development strategies can help you acquire new skills and knowledge, increase your productivity, and achieve your goals. Remember, self-improvement is a continuous process.

PART 3

Attain Your Desire

"Whatever the mind can conceive and believe, it can achieve."
Napoleon Hill

Tracking your progress can be like trying to catch a greased pig at a county fair.

Chapter 16

Assessing Your Progress: Key Performance Indicators and Metrics

Setting goals and creating action plans are important steps toward achieving your desired outcomes, but how do you know if you're making progress? Ah, the elusive art of progress tracking—it's like trying to catch a greased pig at a county fair. In this chapter, we'll explore the wonderful world of Key Performance Indicators (KPIs) and metrics. Think of them as your trusty GPS on the road to success—they'll guide you, keep you on track, and prevent you from ending up in a ditch. From choosing the right KPIs for your goals, to using them to assess your progress, we'll cover it all. Let's look deeper at how you can move forward to achieving your desired outcome.

What are Key Performance Indicators and Metrics?

KPIs and metrics are measurements that help you track your progress toward your goals. KPIs are specific, measurable, and relevant indicators of how well you are achieving your objectives. Metrics, on the other hand, are quantitative measurements of your progress. Both KPIs and metrics are important tools for assessing your progress toward your goals.

Here's an example. Let's say you want to increase the sales of your Aunt Mildred's BBQ sauce, which you started bottling and selling in artisan shops. Last year, much to Aunt Mildred's joy, you sold $90,000 worth, but your *target* sales were $100,000. This year you want to increase that 10%. To find your KPI on sales, you'd use this formula: ACTUAL VALUE/TARGET VALUE x 100 = KPI. So it would be $90,000/$100,000 x 100= 90%. You hit 90% of your target sales.

Your metrics would be the actual amount of jars you sold per month, for example.

Choosing the Right KPIs and Metrics

Choosing the right KPIs and metrics is crucial to accurately measure your progress. You want to choose KPIs and metrics that are relevant to your goals and provide meaningful insight into your progress. Here are some factors to consider when choosing KPIs and metrics:

- *Relevance:* Your KPIs and metrics should be relevant to your goals. For example, if your goal is to increase sales, your KPIs and metrics should measure sales performance.
- *Specificity:* Your KPIs and metrics should be specific and clearly defined. For example, instead of using a general metric like "customer satisfaction," use a

specific metric like "Net Promoter Score" to measure customer loyalty.

- *Actionability:* Your KPIs and metrics should provide actionable insight. For example, if your KPI is to reduce customer churn rate, you should also track the reasons why customers are leaving so you can take action to address those issues.
- *Measurability:* Your KPIs and metrics should be measurable. For example, if your KPI is to increase employee productivity, you should be able to measure productivity using a specific metric like "the number of tasks completed per hour."
- *Timeliness:* Your KPIs and metrics should be timely. For example, if your goal is to reduce customer response time, you should measure response time on a daily or weekly basis to identify any issues as soon as possible.

KPIs are more critical in some industries than others. As you can imagine, the finance industry is especially interested in meticulously tracking moves before making big investments or stock trades, especially if handling someone else's money. Other industries that greatly benefit from KPIs are the retail industry, the manufacturing industry, the shipping and logistics industries and the travel and tourism industries. Let's take a closer look at that last one to give you an idea of some KPIs.

Case Study: The Travel Industry

We'll say that you own Visit Rome Tours, and you provide a vacations for people who want to see Rome, Italy. You take them to all of the tourist traps, but also provide some authentic, local experiences and know the best restaurants squirreled away for them to dine in. Imagine how many things there would be to keep track of! It would be easy to get caught up in the fact that the trip went well (or didn't!) and not measure all of the small things that can add up to your company making it or failing. Here are some things that someone in the travel industry who books tours might use as their KPIs:

- Average booking value
- Customer acquisition cost (Ads, etc.)
- Online Reviews and Ratings
- Website Traffic and Conversion rate
- Customer Lifetime value

The metrics they might keep track of are:
- Average booking window time
- Average trip price per person
- Overall spend

By keeping track of the above, they can figure out if they are charging the right price, if they're allowing enough time to book, and if they are spending too much on advertising.

They can also follow their reviews and ratings to figure out what to improve on for the next tour.

Case Study: Olympian Simone Biles

Simone Biles is an Olympic gymnast who has won numerous medals and is considered one of the greatest gymnasts of all time. Throughout her career, Biles has set and achieved many goals, including winning four gold medals at the 2016 Rio Olympics. Biles has also used KPIs and metrics to track her progress and assess her performance.

For example, she has used a training tracker to monitor her progress and identify areas for improvement. She has been known to practice six hours each day, and this includes strength training, circuit training, endurance training, and of course, gymnastics. That's a lot to keep track of. Time. Weight or resistance bands. Number of reps, etc. Biles has worked with coaches and trainers to develop KPIs and metrics that are specific to her goals, such as increasing her difficulty score on certain routines. By using KPIs and metrics, Biles has been able to make data-driven decisions and continuously improve her performance, which has helped her achieve her desired outcomes.

Biles is also a journaler and writes her goals out on paper. She sets her intentions for the day, for the week, for the month, and overall for the year. Her original goal was relatively modest, to make a college gymnastics team. But as she tracked her program, and grew stronger and more talented, she realized she could do gymnastics full time. She used KPIs and metrics to gradually increase her gym time throughout the physical changes in her body as she matured, as well as using them to balance her mental and physical health and change some of her long-term goals.

Conclusion

In conclusion, KPIs and metrics are essential tools for assessing progress toward your goals. By choosing the right KPIs and metrics, you can track your progress, identify areas for improvement, and make data-driven decisions to achieve your desired outcomes. Whether you're a business owner, athlete, artist, scientist, or social activist, KPIs, and metrics can help you stay focused and motivated as you work towards your goals.

Battling the forces of procrastination, perfectionism, and self-sabotage can be like trying to navigate a minefield while wearing clown shoes.

Chapter 17

Overcoming Obstacles: Procrastination, Perfectionism, and Self-Sabotage

There's the eternal struggle of trying to achieve our goals while simultaneously battling the forces of procrastination, perfectionism, and self-sabotage. It's like trying to navigate a minefield while wearing clown shoes—a precarious situation, to say the least. In this chapter, we'll explore the art of overcoming these obstacles and reaching your desired outcomes. From time-management tips to embracing imperfection, we'll cover it all. So let's put on those clown shoes and get ready to conquer the minefield of success!

Understanding Procrastination

Procrastination is the act of delaying or postponing tasks. It's a common phenomenon that affects many people, and it can be a significant obstacle to achieving our goals. Procrastination can occur for a variety of reasons, including:

- Fear of failure or success
- Feeling overwhelmed

- Lack of motivation
- Poor time management skills

Whatever the reason, procrastination can lead to missed opportunities, increased stress, and a lack of progress toward our goals. So, how can we overcome procrastination?

Practical Exercise: Overcoming Procrastination

Here are some practical steps you can take to overcome procrastination:

- *Identify the root cause:* Take some time to reflect on why you are procrastinating. Is it due to fear, overwhelm, lack of motivation, or something else?
- *Break it down:* If you're feeling overwhelmed by a task, break it down into smaller, more manageable steps. This can help make the task feel less daunting.
- *Create a plan:* Make a plan for how you will tackle the task. Set specific, achievable goals and create a timeline for completing each step.
- *Get started:* Sometimes, the hardest part is getting started. Set a timer for 25 minutes and commit to working on the task for that amount of time. Once you get started, you may find that it's easier to keep going.
- *Eliminate distractions:* Turn off your phone, close your email, and eliminate other distractions that may be tempting you to procrastinate.

Understanding Perfectionism

Perfectionism is the tendency to set high standards for oneself and to strive for flawlessness. While setting high standards can be a positive thing, perfectionism can also be an obstacle to achieving our goals. Perfectionism can lead to the following:

- Fear of failure
- Procrastination
- Stress and anxiety
- Missed opportunities

In fact, studies have shown that perfectionism is associated with a range of negative outcomes, including burnout and mental health problems such as anxiety and depression. Therefore, it's important to learn how to manage perfectionism and strive for excellence without letting it become a hindrance to our progress.

Practical Exercise: Overcoming Perfectionism

Here are some practical steps you can take to overcome perfectionism:

- *Recognize the difference between excellence and perfection:* Perfectionism is often driven by a belief that anything less than perfect is unacceptable. However, it's important to recognize that there is a difference between striving for excellence and striving for perfection. Excellence is about doing your best and continuously improving, while perfection is an unattainable standard.

- *Set realistic expectations:* Setting unrealistic expectations for ourselves can set us up for failure and perpetuate our perfectionism. Instead, set realistic expectations that challenge you but are also achievable.
- *Celebrate progress:* Instead of focusing only on the end result, celebrate your progress along the way. Recognize and appreciate your accomplishments, even if they're not perfect.
- *Practice self-compassion:* Treat yourself with kindness and understanding, especially when you make mistakes or fall short of your own expectations. Remember that making mistakes is a natural part of the learning process.

Fear of Failure

The fear of failure can prevent action by creating a mental barrier that stops people from trying new things or taking risks. This fear can be paralyzing, leading individuals to avoid situations that may challenge their abilities or expose them to the possibility of failure.

The fear of failure can arise from a variety of sources, including past experiences, societal pressures, and personal insecurities. For example, a person who has experienced failure in the past may be reluctant to try again for fear of repeating the same outcome. Similarly, societal expectations and the pressure to succeed can create a sense of anxiety around failure, causing people to avoid taking risks.

When people are consumed by the fear of failure, they may become trapped in a cycle of inaction. They may avoid opportunities that could lead to personal growth and development and miss out on the chance to achieve their goals. This can lead to feelings of frustration, regret, and a sense of unfulfilled potential.

Practical Exercise: Overcoming Fear of Failure

Here are some practical steps you can take to overcome fear of failure:

- *Recognize that failure is a natural part of the learning process.* It's through failure that we learn what doesn't work and gain valuable experience that can help us succeed in the future. Instead of viewing failure as a negative outcome, reframe it as a steppingstone to success.
- *Set realistic expectations and focus on the process rather than the outcome* By breaking down larger goals into smaller, more manageable steps, we can build momentum and gain confidence in our abilities. Celebrating small successes along the way can also help reinforce positive behavior and build self-esteem.
- *Seek support from others* This can be a valuable tool in overcoming the fear of failure. Surrounding

ourselves with people who encourage and support us can help boost our confidence and provide a sense of accountability. Seeking out mentors or joining a supportive community can also provide valuable guidance and resources for overcoming obstacles and achieving our goals.

The fear of failure can be a powerful barrier to action, preventing people from reaching their full potential. By reframing failure as a natural part of the learning process, setting realistic expectations, focusing on the process, and seeking support from others, we can break free of the fear of failure and take meaningful action towards our goals.

Self-Sabotage

We be admis if we didn't take a look at Self-Sabotage in this chapter. Self-sabotage is the act of undermining one's own efforts toward achieving a goal. It can happen consciously or unconsciously, so it's important that you are aware of it so you can spot it before it derails you. There are many reasons people self-sabotage, but they are usually tied in with feels of anxiety, worthlessness or anger. For example, if your boss has cut you and your work down in front of others, you may turn in an unfinished or badly written report due to anger or feelings of incompetence.

Self-sabotage can manifest in a variety of ways, including:

- Procrastination

- Negative self-talk
- Doubting oneself
- Engaging in self-destructive behaviors

Self-sabotage can be a significant obstacle to achieving our goals, as it can prevent us from taking action toward our desired outcomes. Therefore, it's important to recognize when we are engaging in self-sabotage and learn how to overcome it.

Practical Exercise: Overcoming Self-Sabotage

Here are some practical steps you can take to overcome self-sabotage:

- *Identify patterns of self-sabotage:* Take some time to reflect on when and how you engage in self-sabotage. What triggers your self-sabotage? What are the consequences of your self-sabotage?
- *Challenge negative self-talk:* Pay attention to the negative self-talk that may be contributing to your self-sabotage. Challenge these. A good way to start is by not saying something to yourself that you wouldn't say to someone you care about.

Case Study: Vincent Van Gogh

    The renowned artist Vincent Van Gogh struggled with both procrastination and perfectionism throughout his artistic career. He often put off painting, waiting for inspiration to strike, and would become overly self-critical of his work. Despite his struggles, Van Gogh continued to pursue his passion for art and developed a unique style that inspired generations of artists.

To overcome procrastination, Van Gogh developed a routine of painting every day, even if he didn't feel inspired. He believed that practice was essential for improving his skills and creating new ideas. Additionally, he sought out support from other artists, including Paul Gauguin, who challenged him to experiment with new techniques and styles.

To manage his perfectionism, Van Gogh learned to recognize the difference between excellence and perfection. He strove to create works that were expressive and emotional rather than flawless and technically perfect. He also learned to celebrate his progress rather than focusing solely on the end result.

Despite his struggles with procrastination and perfectionism, Van Gogh's commitment to his craft and willingness to seek out support and manage his perfectionism led to a legacy of inspiring and influential art.

Conclusion

Managing procrastination, perfectionism and self-sabotage are important skills to develop in order to achieve our goals and maintain our mental health and well-being. Perfectionism, if left unchecked, can lead to burnout and negative mental health outcomes, while self-sabotage can prevent us from taking action toward our desired outcomes. By recognizing the difference between excellence and perfection, setting realistic expectations, celebrating progress, and practicing self-compassion, we can learn to manage our perfectionism. Ultimately, developing these skills can lead to greater success, happiness, and fulfillment in both our personal and professional lives.

Chapter 18

Facing Your Fears: Failure, Rejection, and Criticism

The sweet sound of fear—the familiar melody that plays in the minds of those who dare to dream big. Fear of failure, rejection, and criticism can be like clingy exes that just won't let go. In this chapter we'll discuss how to face these fears head-on and turn them into opportunities for growth and development. From embracing failure to dealing with rejection, we'll cover it all. So buckle up and let's conquer that fear together.

Recognizing the Value of Failure, Rejection, and Criticism

Before we dive into strategies for facing our fears, it's important to recognize the value of failure, rejection, and criticism. While they can be uncomfortable and even painful experiences, they can also provide valuable opportunities for growth and learning.

Failure: Failure is an inevitable part of the learning process. When we fail, we have the opportunity to reflect on what went wrong and make improvements for next time. Many successful people have experienced multiple failures before achieving their goals, including Thomas Edison, who famously said, "I have not failed. I've just found 10,000 ways that won't work."

Rejection: Rejection can be difficult to handle, but it's important to recognize that it's not a reflection of our worth or abilities. It's simply a decision that someone else has made based on their own needs and preferences. Rejection can provide us with opportunities to reflect on our approach and make improvements for next time.

Criticism: Criticism can be tough to hear, but it can also provide valuable insights and feedback that can help us improve. By taking criticism in stride and using it to make positive changes, we can become more resilient and better equipped to handle future challenges.

Practical Exercise: Reframing Failure, Rejection, and Criticism

Here are some practical steps you can take to reframe your perspective on failure, rejection, and criticism:

- *Acknowledge the value:* Recognize that failure, rejection, and criticism can provide valuable opportunities for growth and learning.
- *Reflect on past experiences:* Think about a time when you experienced failure, rejection, or criticism. How did you handle it? What did you learn from the experience?

- *Reframe your thoughts:* Challenge negative thoughts about failure, rejection, and criticism. Instead, focus on the potential for growth and learning that these experiences provide.

Facing Your Fears

Now that we've explored the value of failure, rejection, and criticism, let's dive into strategies for facing our fears head-on.

- *Identify your fears:* The first step in facing your fears is to identify them. What are you afraid of? Is it a failure, rejection, criticism, or something else?
- *Explore the root cause:* Once you've identified your fears, take some time to explore the root cause. What experiences or beliefs may be contributing to your fears? For example, if you're afraid of failure, is it because you've had negative experiences with failure in the past?
- *Challenge your beliefs:* Often, our fears are based on limiting beliefs that aren't necessarily true. Challenge these beliefs by asking yourself if they are based on facts or assumptions.
- *Take small steps:* Facing your fears can be overwhelming, so it's important to take small steps. Start with something that feels manageable, and work your way up.

Practical Exercise: Facing Your Fears

Here are some practical steps you can take to face your fears:

- *Create a plan:* Write down specific steps you can take to face your fears. Break down larger goals into smaller, more manageable steps.
- *Visualize success:* Take some time to visualize yourself overcoming your fears and achieving your goals. This can help you build confidence and motivation.
- *Practice self-compassion:* Remember that facing your fears is a difficult and often uncomfortable process. Be kind and compassionate to yourself throughout the process.

Now, let's take a look at the fear of failure, rejection and criticism in more detail.

Fear of Failure

The fear of failure can prevent action by creating a mental barrier that stops people from trying new things or taking risks. This fear can be paralyzing, leading individuals to avoid situations that may challenge their abilities or expose them to the possibility of failure.

The fear of failure can arise from a variety of sources, including past experiences, societal pressures, and personal insecurities. For example, a person who has experienced failure in the past may be reluctant to try again for fear of repeating the same outcome. Similarly, societal expectations and the pressure to succeed can create a sense of anxiety around failure, causing people to avoid taking risks.

When people are consumed by the fear of failure, they may become trapped in a cycle of inaction. They may avoid opportunities that could lead to personal growth and development and miss out on the chance to achieve their goals. This can lead to feelings of frustration, regret, and a sense of unfulfilled potential.

Practical Exercise: Overcoming Fear of Failure

Here are some practical steps you can take to overcome fear of failure:

- *Recognize that failure is a natural part of the learning process.* It's through failure that we learn what doesn't work and gain valuable experience that can help us succeed in the future. Instead of viewing failure as a negative outcome, reframe it as a steppingstone to success.
- *Set realistic expectations and focus on the process rather than the outcome* By breaking down larger goals into smaller, more manageable steps, we can build momentum and gain confidence in our abilities. Celebrating small successes along the way can also help reinforce positive behavior and build self-esteem.

- *Seek support from others* This can be a valuable tool in overcoming the fear of failure. Surrounding ourselves with people who encourage and support us can help boost our confidence and provide a sense of accountability. Seeking out mentors or joining a supportive community can also provide valuable guidance and resources for overcoming obstacles and achieving our goals.

The fear of failure can be a powerful barrier to action, preventing people from reaching their full potential. By reframing failure as a natural part of the learning process, setting realistic expectations, focusing on the process, and seeking support from others, we can break free of the fear of failure and take meaningful action towards our goals.

Handling Rejection and Criticism

While facing your fears can be a powerful tool for achieving your goals, it's important to also know how to handle rejection and criticism in a healthy way.

Here are some strategies for handling rejection and criticism:

- *Don't take it personally:* Remember that rejection and criticism are not a reflection of your worth or abilities. It's simply a decision or feedback that someone else has made based on their own needs and preferences.
- *Take time to process:* Give yourself time to process and reflect on the rejection or criticism. It's okay to

feel upset or disappointed, but try not to dwell on it for too long.
- *Seek feedback:* If possible, seek feedback on how you can improve. This can help you turn rejection or criticism into a learning opportunity.
- *Move forward:* Once you've processed the rejection or criticism, try to move forward. Take what you've learned and use it to make positive changes in the future.

Practical Exercise: Handling Rejection and Criticism

While facing your fears can be a powerful tool for achieving your goals, it's important to also know how to handle rejection and criticism in a healthy way.

Here are some strategies for handling rejection and criticism:

- *Take time to process:* Give yourself time to process and reflect on the rejection or criticism. It's okay to feel upset or disappointed but try not to dwell on it for too long.
- *Practice self-compassion:* Remember to be kind and compassionate to yourself throughout the process. Don't beat yourself up over a rejection or criticism.
- *Seek feedback:* If possible, seek feedback on how you can improve. This can help you turn rejection or criticism into a learning opportunity.

- *Focus on the positive:* While it can be difficult to see the positive in a rejection or criticism, try to focus on any feedback or opportunities for growth.
- *Don't take it personally:* Remember that rejection and criticism are not a reflection of your worth or abilities. It's simply a decision or feedback that someone else has made based on their own needs and preferences.
- *Move forward:* Once you've processed the rejection or criticism, try to move forward. Take what you've learned and use it to make positive changes in the future.

Managing procrastination, perfectionism and self-sabotage are important skills to develop in order to achieve our goals and maintain our mental health and well-being.

Case Study: Oprah Winfrey

Oprah Winfrey is a media mogul, philanthropist, and actress who has overcome significant challenges and setbacks on her journey to success. One notable example of this is when she was fired from her job as a television anchor early in her career. This experience could have led her to give up on her dreams, but instead, she chose to use it as an opportunity for growth and reflection. Oprah's success is a testament to her ability to face and overcome her fears of failure, rejection, and criticism.

After being fired, Oprah didn't wallow in self-pity or allow the rejection to define her. Instead, she took the time to reflect on what went wrong and how she could improve. She recognized that she had been too focused on reading the news rather than connecting with her audience, and she used this insight to improve her approach.

Oprah's willingness to face rejection and use it as an opportunity for growth paid off. She went on to become the host of her own talk show, *The Oprah Winfrey Show*, which became one of the most successful and influential shows in television history. Her show tackled important social and cultural issues, and Oprah's ability to connect with her audience and offer them hope and inspiration helped to make her a beloved figure around the world.

Despite her enormous success, Oprah has also faced criticism and negative feedback throughout her career. Some have accused her of promoting "new age" spirituality, while others have criticized her for her involvement in various controversies. However, she has always been willing to face this criticism head-on and use it as an opportunity for growth and reflection.

For example, in the 1990s, Oprah faced criticism for featuring guests who claimed to have recovered memories of childhood sexual abuse. Some accused her of promoting false memories and contributing to a "witch hunt" against innocent people. Oprah faced this criticism head-on, inviting skeptics and critics onto her show to offer their perspective. She also began to feature more balanced discussions of controversial topics and to emphasize the importance of skepticism and critical thinking.

Overall, Oprah's ability to face her fears of failure, rejection, and criticism has been a key factor in her success. By using these experiences as opportunities for growth and reflection, she has been able to overcome setbacks and challenges and to become one of the most influential figures of our time.

Case Study: Author J.K. Rowling

J.K. Rowling's journey to success is one that is truly inspiring. Despite her undeniable talent as a writer, she faced rejection time and time again before finally achieving recognition with her Harry Potter series. Receiving rejection letters from 12 different publishers could have easily discouraged anyone, but not Rowling. She persevered and continued to refine her craft, refusing to let the fear of failure and rejection defeat her.

Rowling's story is a testament to the fact that facing our fears can be the key to achieving remarkable success. It takes immense courage to continue pursuing a dream in the face of rejection and criticism, but Rowling's determination paid off in the end. Her ability to face and overcome her fears allowed her to not only achieve her own personal goals, but also to inspire countless others to do the same.

In today's fast-paced and often competitive world, it can be easy to become discouraged by setbacks and failures. However, Rowling's story serves as a reminder that success often requires us to confront our fears head on. Whether it's fear of failure, rejection, or criticism, learning to face and overcome these challenges can be the key to achieving our goals and realizing our full potential.

Overall, J.K. Rowling's journey serves as a powerful example of the importance of perseverance, determination, and the courage to face our fears. Her story should inspire us all to continue pursuing our dreams, even when the odds seem stacked against us.

Case Study: Superstar Michael Jordan

Michael Jordan is a basketball icon, widely hailed as one of the greatest players of all time. But what many may not know is that his road to success was paved with setbacks and failures.

In high school, Jordan was initially cut from the basketball team. This rejection could have deterred him, but he chose to use it as motivation to improve his skills. In college, he faced another setback when he missed a game-winning shot in the NCAA championship game. This failure could have crushed his confidence, but instead, he used it as a learning experience and as fuel to work even harder.

Even after Jordan achieved success in the NBA, he faced further obstacles. He suffered a serious foot injury that kept him out for most of his second season. But he didn't let this setback stop him. Instead, he focused on his rehabilitation and came back even stronger, leading his team to the playoffs.

Jordan's resilience in the face of failure and criticism is a powerful example of how to handle rejection and setbacks in a healthy way. He never gave up, always worked hard, and used his setbacks as motivation to become a better player and person.

Conclusion

Facing your fears of failure, rejection, and criticism can be a difficult and uncomfortable process, but it's also essential for achieving your goals and reaching your full potential. By recognizing the value of these experiences, reframing your thoughts, and taking small steps, you can overcome your fears and achieve great success. And remember, when faced with rejection or criticism, use it as an opportunity for growth and improvement.

Chapter 19

Learning from Feedback: Feedback Loops, Surveys, and Reviews

Feedback is a crucial aspect of personal and professional growth. It helps us identify areas of improvement and build upon our strengths. As discussed in the previous chapter, the fear of failure, rejection and criticism can hold you back. But, if you are willing to receive constructive feedback (and sometimes even not so constructive!), it can offer you an advantage.

Whether it's from our boss, our peers, or our customers, feedback is the key ingredient to personal and professional growth. From surveys to reviews, we will explore the various ways in which feedback can be gathered and utilized to drive success. By learning how to effectively receive and utilize feedback, we can continuously improve ourselves and our work, ultimately leading to greater success and fulfillment. In this chapter, we will delve into the importance of feedback, the different types of feedback loops, and how to use feedback to enhance our skills and performance.

The Importance of Feedback

Feedback is essential for growth and development. It helps us identify areas of improvement and build upon our strengths. Feedback can come in many forms, including constructive criticism, positive reinforcement, and suggestions for improvement. Without feedback, we may not be aware of areas where we need to improve or how to build upon our strengths.

The Benefits of Feedback

Receiving feedback has many benefits, including:

- *Increased self-awareness:* Feedback can help us gain a better understanding of our strengths and weaknesses.
- *Improved performance:* Feedback can help us identify areas of improvement and make positive changes to enhance our skills and performance.
- *Better communication:* Feedback can improve communication between individuals or teams by creating a space for open dialogue and sharing.
- *Increased motivation:* Positive feedback can boost our confidence and motivation to continue working towards our goals.

Types of Feedback Loops

There are different types of feedback loops that can be used to gather feedback. Here are some of the most common types:

- *Self-Assessment:* This involves reflecting on your own performance and identifying areas where you need to improve.
- *Peer Feedback:* This involves receiving feedback from colleagues or peers who have observed your performance.
- *Supervisor Feedback:* This involves receiving feedback from a supervisor or manager who has observed your performance.
- *Customer Feedback:* This involves gathering feedback from customers or clients to improve products or services.
- *360-Degree Feedback:* This involves receiving feedback from multiple sources, including peers, supervisors, subordinates, and customers.

Practical Exercise: Identifying Feedback Sources

Here are some practical steps you can take to identify sources of feedback:

- *Identify your goals:* Identify the goals you want to achieve and the skills or areas where you want to improve.
- *Identify potential feedback sources:* These could include colleagues, supervisors, customers, and peers.
- *Determine the most effective feedback sources:* Determine which feedback sources will be the most effective in helping you achieve your goals.

Using Feedback to Improve Performance

Receiving feedback is one thing but using it to improve performance is another. Here are some practical steps you can take to use feedback to enhance your skills and performance:

- *Review feedback objectively:* When receiving feedback, it's important to review it objectively without taking it personally or becoming defensive.
- *Identify patterns:* Look for patterns in feedback to identify areas where you need to improve.
- *Set goals:* Use feedback to set goals for improvement, focusing on specific areas where you want to make positive changes.
- *Develop an action plan:* Develop an action plan that outlines the steps you need to take to achieve your goals.
- *Monitor progress:* Monitor your progress regularly to ensure that you are on track to achieve your goals.

Practical Exercise: Creating an Action Plan

Here are some practical steps you can take to create an action plan:

- *Identify your goals:* Identify the areas where you want to improve and set specific goals for improvement.
- *Identify action steps:* Determine the action steps you need to take to achieve your goals.

- *Establish timelines:* Establish realistic timelines for achieving your goals and completing the action steps.
- *Assign responsibilities:* Identity who will be responsible for each action step.
- *Monitor progress:* Regularly monitor your progress towards achieving your goals and completing the action steps.

Using Surveys and Reviews for Feedback

Surveys and reviews are another powerful tool for gathering feedback. They can be used to gather feedback from customers, employees, or other stakeholders. Here are some tips for using surveys and reviews effectively:

- *Be specific:* When creating a survey or review, be specific in your questions to gather meaningful feedback.
- *Keep it simple:* Keep the survey or review simple and easy to understand to encourage more responses.
- *Encourage honesty:* Encourage honesty in feedback by assuring respondents that their feedback will be taken seriously and used to make improvements.
- *Act on feedback:* Use feedback to make positive changes and improvements to products, services, or processes.

Practical Exercise: Creating a Customer Feedback Survey

Here are some practical steps you can take to create a customer feedback survey:

- *Identify the goal of the survey:* Determine what specific information you want to gather from customers.
- *Determine the questions:* Develop specific questions that will help you gather the information you need.
- *Choose a platform:* Choose a platform for hosting the survey, such as SurveyMonkey or Google Forms.
- *Distribute the survey:* Distribute the survey to your customer base through email or social media.
- *Analyze the results:* Analyze the results of the survey and use the feedback to make improvements to products, services, or processes.

Feedback is a crucial aspect of personal and professional growth.

THE POWER OF DESIRE — WES BERRY

Case Study: Michael Phelps

Michael Phelps' remarkable achievements as an Olympic swimmer were made possible by his unwavering dedication to improving his performance through feedback. Phelps recognized the importance of feedback loops, surveys, and reviews in helping him identify areas of improvement and drive his success.

One of the most significant examples of Phelps' commitment to feedback was his partnership with his coach. Phelps' coach would film his swim meets and provide feedback on his technique, allowing him to see firsthand where he could make improvements. Phelps would then review the footage, taking note of his coach's observations, and work on making changes to his approach.

Phelps also relied on feedback from his peers and competitors. He would watch videos of his opponents to learn from their techniques and strategies, using this information to improve his own training and preparation.

Additionally, Phelps would regularly seek feedback from his teammates and coaches, asking for their honest assessments of his performance and where he could improve.

The importance of feedback for Phelps was not limited to his training and preparation for competitions. He also recognized the value of feedback in the form of surveys and reviews from his fans and sponsors. Phelps would regularly read feedback from his fans and sponsors, taking note of their opinions and using this information to shape his public persona and brand.

Phelps' commitment to feedback is a true inspiration for anyone striving for excellence in their field. He recognized that feedback, whether from a coach, a competitor, or a fan, is an invaluable tool for identifying areas of improvement and driving success. His dedication to incorporating feedback into his training and preparation, as well as his commitment to listening to his audience and sponsors, set him apart as one of the most successful Olympic swimmers of all time.

Conclusion

Feedback is a powerful tool for personal and professional growth. It helps us identify areas of improvement and build upon our strengths. By using feedback loops, surveys, and reviews, we can gather feedback from multiple sources and use it to enhance our skills and performance. Whether you are an athlete, artist, entrepreneur, or social activist, feedback can help you achieve your goals and reach your full potential.

The secret to success lies in the power of habit formation, routines, and rituals.

Chapter 20

Staying on Track: Habit Formation, Routines, and Rituals

Are you a goal-getters who feels like a hamster on a wheel, spinning round and round with no end in sight? Well, fear, because the secret to success lies in the power of habit formation, routines, and rituals. In this chapter, we'll explore the science behind these powerful tools, and how they can help us stay on track, maintain momentum, and develop a consistent approach toward our desired outcomes. We'll examine the benefits they can bring to our lives, and how to develop effective habits that will help us achieve our wildest dreams.

Forget the days of constantly battling the snooze button or forgetting to eat breakfast. With effective habit formation, you'll be a well-oiled machine, effortlessly achieving your goals like a boss. And who doesn't love a good routine or ritual? They add a little spice to our day-to-day lives and can help us feel more in control and less like we're drowning in a sea of chaos.

Let's dive in!

The Science of Habit Formation

Habit formation is the process by which new behaviors become automatic. Habits are formed when we repeat an action regularly, and our brains develop neural pathways that make it easier to perform the action automatically. The science of habit formation involves understanding how the brain works and developing strategies to create new habits effectively.

According to Charles Duhigg, author of the book The *Power of Habit*, habits consist of three parts: a cue, a routine, and a reward. The cue triggers the habit, the routine is the behavior itself, and the reward is the positive outcome that reinforces the habit. Understanding this cycle can aid us in developing effective habits that will help us achieve our goals.

The Benefits of Routines and Rituals

Routines and rituals are structured patterns of behavior that help us stay on track and maintain consistency toward our goals. Routines and rituals have numerous benefits, including:

- *Reduced decision fatigue:* Routines and rituals reduce decision fatigue by creating structure and predictability in our daily lives.
- *Increased productivity:* Routines and rituals create a consistent approach toward our goals.

- *Improved well-being:* Routines and rituals improve well-being by creating a sense of stability and structure in our daily lives.

Types of Routines and Rituals

Different types of routines and rituals can help us achieve our goals. Here are some of the most common types:

- *Morning routine:* A morning routine is a set of habits and behaviors that help us start the day on the right foot. You might get up, brush your teeth, do some yoga, and shower to get your day off right.
- *Work routine:* A work routine is a set of habits and behaviors that help us stay productive and focused during the workday. For example, some people grab a cup of coffee and answer emails first thing in the morning, before they tackle a project.
- *Fitness routine:* A fitness routine is a set of habits and behaviors that help us maintain physical health and well-being. Setting aside a certain time of day or partnering with a friend to keep you motivated are great ways to maintain a fitness routine.
- *Evening routine:* An evening routine is a set of habits and behaviors that help us wind down and prepare for restful sleep. Taking a warm bath or reading a book before bed help a lot of people ease into sleep.

Practical Exercise: Developing Effective Habits

Here are some practical steps you can take to develop effective habits:

- *Identify your goals:* Identify the goals you want to achieve and the habits that will help you achieve them.
- *Start small:* Start with small habits that are easy to implement and build upon them over time.
- *Create a cue:* Create a cue that triggers the habit, such as a specific time of day or a specific action.
- *Develop a routine:* Develop a routine that involves the habit, such as a specific sequence of actions.
- *Establish a reward:* Establish a reward that reinforces the habit, such as a sense of accomplishment or a positive outcome.

Using Routines and Rituals to Achieve Goals

Developing effective routines and rituals can help us stay on track and achieve our goals. Here are some practical steps you can take to use routines and rituals effectively:

- *Identify your goals:* Identify the goals you want to achieve and the routines and rituals that will help you achieve them. We talked about exercise above. Perhaps you want to run a half marathon. You would need to figure out a running plan to build up to it.

- *Develop a routine:* Develop a routine that incorporates the habits and behaviors that will help you achieve your goals. Perhaps go for a run every evening after work.
- *Stick to the routine:* Stick to it consistently, even when challenging or inconvenient.
- *Track your progress:* Keep track of your progress toward your goals and make adjustments to your routine as needed.
- *Celebrate your successes:* Celebrate your successes along the way, whether it's reaching a milestone or sticking to your routine consistently for a certain period.

Case Study: Maya Angelou

Maya Angelou was an American poet, author, and civil rights activist. She was known for her powerful words and her unwavering commitment to social justice. Angelou had a daily routine that involved waking up at 5:30 am, making coffee, and retreating to a hotel room or rented workspace to write. She would work for several hours before taking a break for lunch and spending time with her loved ones. She would then return to work in the afternoon and finish her day by reading and reflecting.

Angelou's routine allowed her to maintain discipline and focus on her craft, even amidst a busy schedule and a demanding career. Her commitment to her routine enabled her to produce some of her most influential works and continue her activism well into her later years.

Conclusion

Habit formation, routines, and rituals are essential tools for achieving our goals. By understanding the science of habit formation and developing effective routines and rituals, we can maintain consistency, increase productivity, and improve our well-being. Maya Angelou demonstrates how developing effective habits can lead to remarkable outcomes. By following practical steps to develop effective habits and using routines and rituals to stay on track, we can realize our desired outcomes and lead fulfilling lives.

Chapter 21

Sustaining Your Momentum: Continuous Improvement and Growth Mindset

Hey there, fellow movers and shakers! Are you tired of feeling like you're stuck in a never-ending game of whack-a-mole, constantly tackling new challenges only to have more pop up in their place? It doesn't have to be that way because the key to sustained success lies in the power of continuous improvement and a growth mindset.

In this chapter, we'll be exploring the importance of keeping up the momentum and continuously improving, even after reaching our desired outcomes. After all, the journey to success is a marathon, not a sprint.

With a growth mindset, we can embrace challenges as opportunities for growth and development, rather than obstacles to be avoided. So, let's strap on our running shoes and dive into the world of continuous improvement and a growth mindset. We'll explore the benefits they can bring to our lives and how to keep the momentum going long after we cross the finish line. Get ready to crush those goals and leave those pesky moles in the dust!

Continuous Improvement

Continuous improvement is the process of constantly refining and improving our skills, knowledge, and processes. Continuous improvement involves adopting a growth mindset, seeking feedback, and actively seeking opportunities to learn and grow.

One of the most effective ways to practice continuous improvement is through the Kaizen method. Kaizen is a Japanese philosophy that focuses on continuous improvement through small, incremental changes. The Kaizen approach involves breaking down larger goals into smaller, achievable steps and continuously improving upon them.

The Benefits of a Growth Mindset

A growth mindset is a belief that our abilities and intelligence can be developed through dedication and hard work. People with a growth mindset are more likely to embrace challenges, persist through setbacks, and seek out opportunities for learning and growth.

Research has shown that a growth mindset can have numerous benefits, including:

- *Increased resilience:* People with a growth mindset are more resilient and better equipped to handle setbacks and challenges.
- *Improved motivation:* People with a growth mindset are more motivated to learn and grow, leading to higher levels of achievement.

- *Greater creativity:* People with a growth mindset are more likely to think outside the box and explore new ideas and approaches.

Practical Exercise: Embracing a Growth Mindset

Here are some practical steps you can take to embrace a growth mindset:

- *Embrace challenges:* Instead of avoiding challenges, embrace them as opportunities for growth and learning.
- *Seek feedback:* Seek out feedback from others to identify areas for improvement and growth.
- *Learn from mistakes:* Instead of dwelling on mistakes, view them as opportunities for learning and growth.
- *Celebrate progress:* Celebrate small wins and progress towards your goals, no matter how small.

Continuous Improvement Strategies

Here are some strategies to help you practice continuous improvement:

- *Develop a growth mindset:* Embrace a growth mindset and seek out opportunities for learning and growth.
- *Set goals:* Set specific, measurable, and achievable goals that align with your desired outcomes.

- *Seek feedback:* Seek feedback from others to identify areas for improvement and growth.
- *Practice deliberate practice:* Deliberate practice involves breaking down skills into smaller, achievable steps and continuously refining and improving upon them.
- *Reflect on progress:* Regularly reflect on your progress towards your goals and identify areas for improvement.
- *Learn from others:* Seek mentors, coaches, and other experts to learn from their experiences and expertise.

Case Study: Dwayne "The Rock" Johnson

Dwayne "The Rock" Johnson is a former professional wrestler turned actor and producer. He is known for his impressive physique, commanding presence, and charismatic personality. But many people may not know that Johnson is also a great example of someone who sustains his momentum by continuously improving himself and embracing a growth mindset.

Johnson's journey toward success was not an easy one. Growing up, he faced a lot of adversity, including poverty, family problems, and a lack of direction. However, he found solace and inspiration in sports, particularly football, and wrestling. He excelled in both sports and eventually earned a college football scholarship.

After college, Johnson had dreams of playing professional football, but when that didn't work out, he turned to wrestling, following in the footsteps of his father and grandfather. He quickly made a name for himself in the industry, becoming one of the most popular and successful wrestlers of his time.

But Johnson did not rest on his laurels. He knew that to sustain his momentum and continue to grow, he had to improve himself continuously. He trained tirelessly in the gym and the ring, constantly pushing himself to be better and stronger.

Eventually, Johnson transitioned from wrestling to acting, a move that many people doubted he could pull off. But he proved them wrong, starring in blockbuster movies like the *Fast and Furious* franchise, *Jumanji,* and *Moana.* He even created his own production company, Seven Bucks Productions, to help him achieve his creative goals.

Throughout his career, Johnson has embraced a growth mindset, always looking for ways to learn and improve. He is known for his discipline and work ethic, often waking up at 4 a.m. to hit the gym and staying on a strict diet to maintain his physique. He also takes time to reflect on his successes and failures, using them as opportunities to learn and grow.

In interviews, Johnson often talks about the importance of hard work, perseverance, and positivity. He believes that anyone can achieve their goals if they are willing to put in the effort and maintain a growth mindset. His story is an inspiration to many, showing that sustained momentum and growth are achievable through continuous improvement and a mindset that embraces learning and development.

Conclusion

Sustaining momentum and achieving lasting success requires a commitment to continuous improvement and a growth mindset. By embracing challenges, seeking feedback, and actively seeking opportunities to learn and grow, we can develop the skills, knowledge, and mindset needed to achieve our desired outcomes. Remember, success is not a destination, but a journey of continuous improvement and growth.

Chapter 22

Celebrating Your Achievements: Milestone Parties, Gratitude Journals, and Rewards

Attention all high achievers! Are you tired of toiling away in the pursuit of success without taking a moment to celebrate your victories? Well, it's time to break out the confetti and party hats, because celebrating your achievements is crucial to your success. In this chapter, we'll explore the benefits of taking a moment to celebrate your progress—from boosting your motivation to giving you a chance to pat yourself on the back for a job well done. And let's not forget the perks of a good party, am I right? We'll delve into different ways to celebrate, from milestone parties to gratitude journals and even rewards. So, let's raise a glass (or a juice box, if that's more your style) to all the hard work you've put in so far. We'll show you how to incorporate celebration into your goal-setting strategies and keep the momentum going all the way to the finish line. Get ready to party like it's your birthday (even if it's not), because it's time to celebrate your achievements like the rockstar you are!

The Benefits of Celebrating Achievements

Celebrating our achievements has several benefits, including:

- *Increased motivation:* Celebrating our achievements gives us a sense of accomplishment and increases our motivation to continue working towards our goals.
- *Improved self-esteem:* Celebrating our achievements boosts our self-esteem and reinforces the idea that we are capable of achieving our goals.
- *Stress reduction:* Celebrating our achievements can reduce stress and anxiety by giving us a moment to reflect on our progress and feel good about ourselves.

Different Ways to Celebrate

There are different ways to celebrate our achievements, and what works best will depend on personal preferences and circumstances. Here are some examples:

- *Milestone parties:* Celebrating milestones with a party, gathering, or special event is a great way to recognize significant achievements and share the moment with others.
- *Gratitude journals:* Keeping a gratitude journal and reflecting on the progress made towards our goals can be a powerful way to celebrate our achievements and cultivate a positive mindset.
- *Rewards:* Treating ourselves to a reward, such as a special meal, a massage, or a day off, can be a way to

celebrate our achievements and acknowledge the hard work we put in.

Incorporating Celebration into Goal-Setting Strategies

Incorporating celebration into our goal-setting strategies can help us stay motivated and committed to achieving our goals. Here are some practical steps to take:

- *Set milestones:* Break down larger goals into smaller milestones, and celebrate each milestone along the way.
- *Choose meaningful celebrations:* Choose celebrations that are meaningful to you and align with your values and preferences.
- *Reflect on progress:* Take time to reflect on the progress made towards your goals and celebrate the hard work and effort put in.
- *Share the moment:* Share the moment with others who have supported and encouraged you throughout the process.

Practical Exercise: Celebrating Your Achievements

Here's a practical exercise to help you celebrate your achievements:

- *Reflect on your progress:* Take some time to reflect on the progress you have made toward your goals.
- *Identify a milestone:* Identify a significant milestone you have achieved or will soon achieve.

- *Choose a celebration:* Choose a celebration that aligns with your preferences and values.
- *Share the moment:* Share the moment with someone who has supported and encouraged you throughout the process.

Case Study: Serena Williams

Serena Williams' success as a tennis player has been defined by her relentless drive to achieve greatness. However, she also recognizes the importance of celebrating her achievements and taking the time to reflect on her progress.

One of the ways Williams celebrates her milestones is by throwing milestone parties. After her 2017 Australian Open victory, Williams threw a party to celebrate her achievement with her family and team. The party was complete with a specially made cake in the shape of a trophy, reflecting her joy and pride in her hard-earned success.

Williams also rewards herself for her achievements. After winning that same Australian Open in 2017, she treated herself to a well-deserved vacation in the Maldives, where she could relax and enjoy some time off after her intense training and competition schedule.

Additionally, Williams also practices gratitude by keeping a gratitude journal. In interviews, she has shared that she writes down three things she is grateful for every day. This practice helps her focus on the positive aspects of her life and appreciate the many blessings she has received.

Through her dedication to celebrating her achievements, Williams not only demonstrates gratitude for her success but also reinforces the importance of taking time to appreciate the hard work that goes into reaching one's goals. Her example serves as an inspiration for others to take the time to reflect on their progress and celebrate their milestones along the way.

Conclusion

Celebrating our achievements is an essential part of achieving our goals. It helps us stay motivated, boosts our self-esteem, and gives us a moment to reflect on our progress. Incorporating celebration into our goal-setting strategies can be a powerful way to stay committed to our goals and celebrate the hard work and effort we put in. Remember to choose celebrations that align with your preferences and values and share the moment with others who have supported and encouraged you throughout the process.

We can't help everyone, but everyone can help someone.
Ronald Reagan

Chapter 23

Making Your Desired Outcome a Legacy: Giving Back, Paying Forward, and Contributing to Society

As much as we all love achieving our desired outcomes, we have to admit that it's not all about us. We need to think beyond ourselves and consider how we can use our success to make a difference in the world. That's right, it's time to give back, pay it forward, and contribute to society!

In this chapter, we'll explore the benefits of being a do-gooder, from boosting your feel-good vibes to creating a legacy that goes beyond personal success. But we won't just stop at the warm and fuzzy feelings—we'll also discuss practical ways to make a meaningful difference.

We'll show you how to create a legacy that you can be proud of, and how to make a real impact on society. It's time to use our success for good and leave a lasting impression on the world. Are you ready to make a difference? Let's do this!

The Benefits of Giving Back

Giving back to society has numerous benefits, both for the individuals we help and for ourselves. Here are some of the key benefits of giving back and having a sense of purpose:

- *Fulfillment:* Giving back provides a sense of purpose and fulfillment, knowing that we are making a positive impact on the world.
- *Personal growth:* Giving back helps us develop empathy, compassion, and other positive traits that enhance our personal growth and well-being.
- *Social connection:* Giving back fosters social connection and community involvement, which can improve our relationships and sense of belonging.
- *Professional development:* Giving back can enhance our professional skills, such as leadership, communication, and teamwork.

Paying It Forward

Paying it forward is a concept that involves helping others in a way that inspires them to do the same for others. By paying it forward, we create a ripple effect of positive actions that can make a significant difference in the world.

Here are some practical ways to pay it forward:

- *Random acts of kindness:* Perform small acts of kindness for others, such as buying someone's coffee or holding the door open.
- *Volunteering:* Volunteer your time and skills to organizations or causes that you care about.
- *Mentoring:* Share your knowledge and experience with others through mentoring or coaching.
- *Philanthropy:* Make charitable donations to organizations or causes that align with your values.

Contributing to Society

Contributing to society involves using our skills, resources, and influence to create a positive impact on the world. Here are some practical ways to contribute to society:

- *Entrepreneurship:* Use entrepreneurship to create products, services, or solutions that address social or environmental challenges.
- *Social activism:* Engage in social activism and advocacy to promote positive change and advance social justice.
- *Community building:* Create or support initiatives that foster community building, such as neighborhood associations, community gardens, or public art projects.
- *Environmental stewardship:* Take actions to reduce your environmental impact, such as conserving

energy, reducing waste, or supporting renewable energy initiatives.

Case Study: Bill Gates

Bill Gates is widely recognized as one of the most successful entrepreneurs and philanthropists in history. He is the co-founder of Microsoft, and through his charitable organization, the Bill and Melinda Gates Foundation, he has donated billions of dollars to various causes.

One of the Foundation's most notable initiatives has been the fight to eradicate polio. Gates has worked closely with Rotary International, a global organization that promotes peace and fights disease, to raise funds and awareness for the cause. Through the Foundation, Gates has donated over $2 billion towards polio eradication efforts, which has helped to vaccinate millions of children in developing countries.

Beyond polio, the Foundation has focused on a range of other issues, including global health, education, and reducing poverty. Its efforts have led to significant progress in reducing infant mortality rates and increasing access to education in developing countries.

Gates' philanthropic legacy is rooted in his belief that the world's wealthiest individuals are responsible for giving back to society. He has pledged to donate most of his wealth to charity, ensuring that his impact will be felt for generations. His dedication to creating positive change in the world inspires others to follow in his footsteps and use their resources to make a difference in the world.

THE POWER OF DESIRE   WES BERRY

Case Study: Malala Yousafzai

Malala Yousafzai is a powerful example of how one person can make a significant impact in the world by making their desired outcome a legacy. Her story is well-known: at just 15 years old, she was targeted by the Taliban for advocating for girls' education in Pakistan. She survived the assassination attempt and continued to speak out on behalf of education and women's rights.

In 2013, Yousafzai co-founded the Malala Fund with her father, which invests in education programs for girls in developing countries. The organization has funded education programs in countries such as Pakistan, Nigeria, and Kenya, and has helped to provide educational opportunities to thousands of girls who otherwise may not have had access to education. The Malala Fund also advocates for policy changes to improve girls' access to education.

Yousafzai's advocacy work has not gone unnoticed. She has spoken at the United Nations, addressed the Canadian Parliament, and met with leaders from around the world to advocate for girls' education and women's rights. Her inspiring story has inspired millions of people around the world to support education and social justice initiatives.

Yousafzai's legacy is one of determination, resilience, and a commitment to making the world a better place for all. Her advocacy work serves as a reminder that one person, no matter how young or seemingly powerless, can make a significant impact in the world by making their desired outcome a legacy and paying it forward.

Conclusion

In this chapter, we've explored the importance of giving back, paying it forward, and contributing to society. By using our success to create a positive impact on the world, we can leave a lasting legacy that goes beyond personal achievements. Whether it's through philanthropy, social activism, or entrepreneurship, there are numerous ways to make a difference and create a better world for future generations. By practicing the practical exercises in this chapter and reflecting on the case studies of individuals who have made a significant impact on the world, we can be inspired to create our own legacy and make a positive impact on the world.

THE END OF THE BOOK AND THE BEGINNING OF THE CHALLENGE

Turn the page!

21-Day Challenge

Why Accept this Challenge?

There are five main reasons to accept this 21-Day Challenge, particularly one presented by the author of a book you are reading:

1. *Personal growth:* By taking on a challenge, you can push yourself to learn and develop new skills, which can help you grow both personally and professionally.
2. *Improved performance:* A challenge can motivate you to improve your performance and achieve better results, which can benefit both you and your organization.
3. *Increased insight:* A challenge can force you to focus your attention on a specific area, leading to deeper understanding and greater insight. This can help you make more informed decisions and drive innovation in your organization.
4. *Satisfaction of fulfilling a challenging task:* Successfully completing a challenge can give you a sense of accomplishment and satisfaction that comes from overcoming obstacles and achieving a difficult goal. This can boost your confidence and inspire you to take on new challenges in the future.

5. *Mastering the Secret of Desire:* By applying yourself to these challenges you will complete the journey of discovery that is the promise of this book.

Accepting this type of challenge can also provide a unique opportunity to learn from an expert in the field and apply the insights and strategies presented in the book to real-world scenarios. This can help you deepen your understanding of the material and enhance your ability to apply it in your own work.

READ THE CHALLENGE THAN RE-READ THE CORRESPONDING CHAPTER AND BEGIN THE CHALLENGE

Chapter 1 Challenge

Why Desired Outcomes Matter: Unleashing the Power of Vision

Your challenge is to develop a clear and compelling vision of your desired outcome using the five reasons why desired outcomes matter: clarity, motivation, resilience, meaning, and impact. Follow the practical exercises and tips below to create your vision and share it with someone who can provide feedback and support.

1. Reflection: Take time to reflect on your values, passions, and strengths.
2. Visualization: Imagine your ideal future where you have achieved your desired outcome.
3. SMART Goals: Use the SMART criteria to set specific, measurable, achievable, relevant, and time-bound goals.
4. Vision Board: Create a vision board that represents your desired outcome and the things that inspire you.
5. Personal Mission Statement: Write a concise and memorable statement.
6. Get Feedback and Support: Share your vision with someone who can offer you constructive feedback .

Remember that having a clear and compelling vision of your desired outcome can help you overcome confusion, uncertainty, and lack of direction in life.

Notes

Chapter 2 Challenge

The Anatomy of a Desired Outcome: Clarity, Specificity, and Meaning

For this assignment, you are tasked with demonstrating your understanding of "The Anatomy of a Desired Outcome: Clarity, Specificity, and Meaning."

1. Begin by defining each of the three elements: clarity, specificity, and meaning.
2. Provide an example of a desired outcome that lacks clarity, specificity, and meaning.
3. Next, provide an example of a desired outcome that embodies all three elements: clarity, specificity, and meaning.
4. Finally, explain why it is important to have a desired outcome that encompasses all three elements and how you can apply this knowledge in your personal or professional life.

Notes

Chapter 3 Challenge

The Art of Goal-Setting: SMART Criteria and Beyond

For this challenge, you are tasked with demonstrating your understanding of "The Art of Goal-Setting: SMART Criteria."

1. Define each component of the SMART criteria (Specific, Measurable, Achievable, Relevant, and Time-bound).
2. Provide an example of a goal that is not SMART and explain why it fails to meet each of the SMART criteria.
3. Next, provide an example of a goal that is SMART and explain how it meets each of the SMART criteria.
4. Finally, explain how you can apply the SMART criteria to your personal or professional life and why it is important to set SMART goals.

Notes

Chapter 4 Challenge

The Science of Motivation: Intrinsic vs. Extrinsic Drivers

For this assignment, you are tasked with demonstrating your understanding of "The Science of Motivation: Intrinsic vs. Extrinsic Drivers."

1. Define intrinsic and extrinsic drivers of motivation and provide an example of each.
2. Explain the differences between intrinsic and extrinsic motivation, and why they are important to understand.
3. Describe a situation where you were motivated by an intrinsic driver and explain why it was effective.
4. Describe a situation where you were motivated by an extrinsic driver and explain why it was effective.

Finally, explain how you can use this knowledge of intrinsic and extrinsic drivers of motivation to increase your personal or professional motivation.

Notes

Chapter 5 Challenge

The Role of Values, Purpose, and Identity in Desired Outcomes

For this assignment, you are tasked with demonstrating your understanding of "The Role of Values, Purpose, and Identity in Desired Outcomes."

1. Define the concepts of values, purpose, and identity and explain how they are related to each other.
2. Provide an example of a desired outcome that is aligned with your values, purpose, and identity, and explain why it is important to have alignment.
3. Describe a situation where you faced a challenge in achieving a desired outcome that was not aligned with your values, purpose, or identity, and explain how it affected your motivation and satisfaction.
4. Explain how you can use your values, purpose, and identity to set meaningful and authentic goals and increase your motivation and satisfaction in your personal or professional life.

THE POWER OF DESIRE **WES BERRY**

Notes

Chapter 6 Challenge

The Power Trio: Visualization, Affirmation, and Meditation

For this assignment, you are tasked with demonstrating your understanding of "The Importance of Visualization, Affirmation, and Meditation."

1. Define visualization, affirmation, and meditation and explain how they are related to each other.
2. Provide an example of how you have used visualization to enhance your motivation and focus on a desired outcome.
3. Provide an example of how you have used affirmation to boost your confidence and belief in your abilities towards a desired outcome.
4. Explain the benefits of practicing meditation regularly in achieving desired outcomes.

Finally, explain how you can incorporate visualization, affirmation, and meditation into your daily routine to enhance your performance and achieve your desired outcomes.

Notes

Chapter 7 Challenge

The Cognitive Skills, Abilities, and Intuitive Thinking that Drive Success

For this assignment, you are tasked with demonstrating your understanding of "The Cognitive Skills, Abilities, and Intuitive Thinking that Drive Success."

1. Define the cognitive skills, abilities, and intuitive thinking discussed in this lesson and provide examples of each.
2. Explain the importance of critical thinking, problem-solving, and decision-making in achieving success.
3. Describe a situation where you used your cognitive skills to overcome a challenge and achieve a desired outcome.
4. Explain how intuitive thinking can complement analytical thinking and help you make better decisions in complex situations.

Finally, explain how you can develop and improve your cognitive skills and intuitive thinking to enhance your performance and achieve your desired outcomes.

Notes

Chapter 8 Challenge

Positive Thinking:
Unlocking Your Path to Success and Happiness

For this challenge, you are tasked with demonstrating your understanding of "Positive Thinking Delivers Positive Results."

1. Define positive thinking and explain how it differs from negative thinking.
2. Explain how positive thinking can impact our emotions, behaviors, and outcomes in life.
3. Provide an example of a situation where you used positive thinking to overcome a challenge or achieve a desired outcome.
4. Discuss the benefits of practicing positive thinking regularly and how it can contribute to personal growth and success.

Finally, explain how you can incorporate positive thinking into your daily routine to enhance your performance and achieve your desired outcomes.

Notes

Chapter 9 Challenge

Mapping Your Terrain: PESTLE Analysis and Environmental Scanning

For this assignment, you are tasked with demonstrating your understanding of "Mapping Your Terrain: PESTLE Analysis and Environmental Scanning."

1. Define PESTLE analysis and explain how it can be used in strategic planning.
2. Identify the six key components of PESTLE analysis and provide an example of each.
3. Explain the importance of environmental scanning in strategic planning.
4. Provide an example of a situation where you used PESTLE analysis or environmental scanning to inform a business decision.
5. Discuss the limitations of PESTLE analysis and environmental scanning and how they can be overcome.

THE POWER OF DESIRE **WES BERRY**

Notes_____

Chapter 10 Challenge

Developing Your Strategy:
SWOT Matrix

For this assignment, you are tasked with demonstrating your understanding of "Developing Your Strategy: SWOT Matrix."

1. Define SWOT analysis and explain how it can be used in strategic planning.
2. Identify the four key components of SWOT analysis and provide an example of each.
3. Explain the purpose of the SWOT matrix and how it can be used to develop a strategy.
4. Provide an example of a situation where you used the SWOT matrix to inform a business decision.
5. Discuss the limitations of the SWOT matrix and how they can be overcome.

Notes

Chapter 11 Challenge

Developing Your Strategy: Porter's Five Forces

Explain how to utilize Porter's Five Forces framework in developing a business strategy.

1. Begin by providing a brief overview of Porter's Five Forces framework and its purpose in analyzing the competitive forces in an industry.
2. Explain the five forces that are analyzed in the framework, namely: the threat of new entrants, the bargaining power of suppliers, the bargaining power of buyers, the threat of substitutes, and the intensity of competitive rivalry.
3. Demonstrate how to apply the framework in developing a business strategy by providing examples of how each force can be analyzed and addressed.
4. Emphasize the importance of considering all five forces in developing a comprehensive strategy that can effectively address the challenges and opportunities of a particular industry.
5. Conclude by highlighting the potential benefits of utilizing Porter's Five Forces framework in developing a business strategy.

Notes

Chapter 12 Challenge

Creating Your Action Plan: To-Do Lists and Milestones

This is an important stage of your goal-setting journey! It's time to create your real action plan and bring your desired outcomes to life using to-do lists and milestones. Here are the steps to follow:

1. Choose a goal that you want to achieve within the next 3-6 months. Make sure it's specific, measurable, achievable, relevant, and time-bound (SMART).
2. Create a to-do list for each task. Break down each task into smaller, actionable steps and list them in a to-do list. This will help you stay organized and track your progress.
3. Set milestones for your goal. Milestones are specific points in time that mark your progress towards your desired outcome. Identify the key milestones for your goal and set a deadline for each one.
4. Review your action plan regularly. Monitor your progress and make adjustments as needed. Use the Gantt chart, to-do lists, and milestones to stay on track and motivated.

Remember, creating an action plan is an important step towards achieving your goals. By using to-do lists, and milestones, you can break down your goal into manageable steps and track your progress towards your desired outcome. Good luck!

Notes

Chapter 13 Challenge

Building Your Support Network: Mentors, Allies, and Accountability Partners

Building a support network is essential for personal and professional growth. In this challenge, you will learn about the three key types of support in a support network: mentors, allies, and accountability partners.

1. Identify at least three people for each category: mentors, allies, and accountability partners.
2. Reach out to at least one person from each category and ask for their support.
3. Maintain regular contact with your support network and celebrate successes together.
4. Reflect on your progress and identify areas for improvement in your support network.

By completing this challenge, you will learn how to build and nurture a support network to achieve your personal and professional goals.

Notes

Chapter 14

Managing Your Resources: Time, Money, and Energy

Effective resource management is crucial for achieving your desired outcomes. In this challenge, you will learn about the three primary resources you need to manage effectively: time, money, and energy.

1. Read the chapter on "Managing Your Resources: Time, Money, and Energy."
2. Identify your short-term and long-term goals.
3. Assess how you are currently using your time, money, and energy.
4. Develop a resource management plan.
5. Implement and review your resource management plan regularly.
6. Celebrate your successes and identify areas for improvement. Be flexible and make adjustments to your plan as needed. This will help you to stay on track and make sure that you are making progress towards your goals.

Notes

Chapter 15 Challenge

Cultivating Your Skills and Knowledge: Learning Plans and Self-Development

Continuous self-development is crucial for achieving success in today's rapidly changing world. In this challenge, you will learn about the importance of self-development and creating a learning plan that will help you achieve your goals.

1. Identify the skills and knowledge you need to acquire to achieve your short-term and long-term goals.
2. Create a learning plan that outlines how you will acquire the skills and knowledge you need, including resources and timelines.
3. Implement and review your learning plan.
4. Regularly review your progress, celebrating successes and identifying areas for improvement.

Reflect on your learning and how it has impacted your personal and professional growth, considering how you can continue to cultivate your skills and knowledge in the future.

THE POWER OF DESIRE — WES BERRY

Notes

Chapter 16 Challenge

Assessing Your Progress:
Key Performance Indicators and Metrics

In this chapter, you learned about assessing your progress using key performance indicators (KPIs) and metrics. Now, it's time to put that knowledge into practice. Your challenge is to explain how you would utilize what you learned about KPIs and metrics to assess your progress towards a specific goal or objective.

1. Choose a goal or objective that you want to achieve, such as increasing website traffic, improving customer satisfaction, or reducing operating costs. Then, identify the KPIs and metrics that are most relevant to measuring your progress towards that goal.

2. Explain how you would set up a system for tracking and analyzing these KPIs and metrics on a regular basis. Discuss how you would interpret the data to make informed decisions and take action to improve your performance.

3. Be sure to provide specific examples of KPIs and metrics that you would use, as well as any tools or resources that you would need to implement your tracking system.

4. Additionally, explain how you would communicate your progress to stakeholders and adjust your approach as

needed to ensure you stay on track towards achieving your goal.

Notes

Chapter 17 Challenge

Overcoming Obstacles: Procrastination, Perfectionism, and Self-Sabotage

Explain what you have learned about overcoming obstacles such as procrastination, perfectionism, and self-sabotage.

1. Start by summarizing what you learned about each of these obstacles and how they can hold you back from achieving your goals.
2. Next, explain the strategies and techniques you have learned to overcome these obstacles. Provide examples of how you have applied them in your life or how you plan to apply them in the future.
3. Discuss the importance of self-awareness and self-reflection in identifying and addressing these obstacles.

Remember, overcoming these obstacles takes time, effort, and practice. The key is to stay motivated, focused, and persistent in your pursuit of personal growth and achievement.

Notes

Chapter 18

Facing Your Fears: Failure, Rejection, and Criticism

Explain how to utilize what you have learned about facing your fears of failure, rejection, and criticism.

1. Start by summarizing what you learned about each of these fears and how they can hold you back from achieving your goals.
2. Next, explain the strategies and techniques you have learned to face these fears. Provide examples of how you have applied them in your life or how you plan to apply them in the future.
3. Discuss the importance of reframing your mindset and building resilience in order to overcome these fears.
4. Practice these strategies consistently and to seek support from others when necessary.

Remember, facing your fears is a process that requires courage, persistence, and self-compassion. By embracing the challenges that come with failure, rejection, and criticism, you can grow and develop into a more confident and resilient individual.

Notes

Chapter 19 Challenge

Learning from Feedback: Feedback Loops, Surveys, and Reviews

Explain how to utilize what you have learned about learning from feedback through feedback loops, surveys, and reviews.

1. Start by summarizing what you learned about feedback loops, surveys, and reviews, and how they can help you learn and grow.
2. Explain the importance of seeking feedback in different areas of your life, such as work, relationships, and personal development.
3. Emphasize the importance of being open-minded and receptive to feedback, even if it may be difficult to hear.

Remember, learning from feedback is an ongoing process, and requires humility, curiosity, and a willingness to improve. By using feedback loops, surveys, and reviews effectively, you can gain valuable insights that can help you achieve your goals and reach your full potential.

THE POWER OF DESIRE **WES BERRY**

Notes_____

Chapter 20 Challenge

Staying on Track: Habit Formation, Routines, and Rituals

Explain how to utilize what you have learned about staying on track through habit formation, routines, and rituals.

1. Summarize the importance of positive habits and routines.
2. Discuss strategies for forming habits, establishing routines, and developing rituals.
3. Write down some of your own routines and track your progress to see if they are working for you. Remember, consistency is important.

Staying on track requires effort, but by implementing these strategies consistently, you can achieve your goals and live a more fulfilling life.

Notes

Chapter 21 Challenge

Sustaining Your Momentum: Continuous Improvement and Growth Mindset

Explain how you can utilize what you have learned about sustaining your momentum through continuous improvement and growth mindset.

1. Begin by summarizing the key takeaways from the lesson on sustaining your momentum through continuous improvement and growth mindset.
2. Explain how you can apply these concepts to your personal or professional life. Provide specific examples of how you can use continuous improvement and growth mindset to achieve your goals and overcome challenges.
3. Finally, reflect on the benefits of sustaining your momentum through continuous improvement and growth mindset, and how it can contribute to your personal and professional success.

Remember to use clear and concise language and provide specific examples to illustrate your points.

Notes

Chapter 22 Challenge

Celebrating Your Achievements:
Milestone Parties, Gratitude Journals, and Rewards

Here's a practical exercise to help you celebrate your achievements:

1. *Reflect on your progress:* Take some time to reflect on the progress you have made toward your goals.
2. *Identify a milestone:* Identify a significant milestone you have achieved or will soon achieve.
3. *Choose a celebration:* Choose a celebration that aligns with your preferences and values.
4. *Share the moment:* Share the moment with someone who has supported and encouraged you throughout the process.

Notes

Chapter 23 Challenge

Making Your Desired Outcome a Legacy: Giving Back, Paying Forward, and Contributing to Society

Here's a practical exercise to help you create a legacy:
1. Identify a cause or issue that you care about and research organizations or initiatives that work in that area. Consider volunteering your time, skills, or resources to support their work.
2. Reflect on your skills and expertise and consider how you can use them to address social or environmental challenges. Brainstorm ideas for products, services, or solutions that can positively impact the world.
3. Practice paying it forward by performing small acts of kindness for others. Consider keeping a gratitude journal to reflect on the positive impact of your actions.
5. Consider the legacy you want to leave behind and how you can use your success to create a lasting impact. Reflect on the values and causes that are important to you and identify ways to incorporate them into your personal and professional life.

THE POWER OF DESIRE　　　　　　　　WES BERRY

Notes_____

THE POWER OF DESIRE   WES BERRY

Dear Readers,

As I come to the end of this book, I want to take a moment to express my deepest gratitude to you. Your support, interest, and enthusiasm for my work have meant the world to me. Writing can be a solitary pursuit, but knowing that there are readers out there who are engaged with my words and ideas has been a constant source of inspiration and motivation.

I also want to thank those who have helped me along the way - my family, friends, and colleagues who have provided encouragement, feedback, and support. Without you, this book would not have been possible.

Finally, I want to thank you for taking the time to read this book. I hope it was informative and even inspired you to achieve your desired goals. It has been a joy and an honor to share this journey with you, and I look forward to continuing it together.

With gratitude,

Wes

PS: You have the tools, now get to work!

THE POWER OF DESIRE

WES BERRY

References

Chapter 1. Why Desired Outcomes Matter: The Power of Vision
Covey, S. R. (2004). The 7 habits of highly effective people: Powerful lessons in personal change. Simon and Schuster.

Locke, E. A., & Latham, G. P. (2002). Building a practically useful theory of goal setting and task motivation: A 35-year odyssey. American Psychologist, 57(9), 705-717.

Marques, J. F. (2010). The psychology of meaning in life. Nova Science Publishers.

Ryan, R. M., & Deci, E. L. (2000). Self-determination theory and the facilitation of intrinsic motivation, social development, and well-being. American Psychologist, 55(1), 68-78.

Sinek, S. (2009). Start with why: How great leaders inspire everyone to take action. Penguin.

Virgin Group. (2021). About Us. Retrieved from https://www.virgin.com/about-us.

Billionaire Richard Branson: 'I didn't start Virgin to make money. Clifford, Catherine. MakeIt (21 May, 2019). Accessed at: https://www.cnbc.com/2019/05/21/billionaire-richard-branson-i-didnt-start-virgin-to-make-money.html#:~:text="I%20didn%27t%20start%20Virgin,which%20developed%20into%20Virgin%20Records.

Chapter 2: The Anatomy of a Desired Outcome: Clarity, Specificity, and Meaning
Covey, S. R. (2004). The 7 Habits of Highly Effective People: Powerful Lessons in Personal Change. Simon and Schuster.

Doran, G. T. (1981). There's a S.M.A.R.T. way to write management's goals and objectives. Management Review, 70(11), 35-36.

Locke, E. A., & Latham, G. P. (2002). Building a practically useful theory of goal setting and task motivation: A 35-year odyssey. American Psychologist, 57(9), 705-717.

Pink, D. H. (2009). Drive: The Surprising Truth About What Motivates Us. Riverhead Books.

Robinson, K. (2006). The Element: How Finding Your Passion Changes Everything. Penguin.

Sinek, S. (2009). Start with Why: How Great Leaders Inspire Everyone to Take Action. Portfolio.
Smart, J., & Street, E. (2006). The Essential Guide to Managing Small Business Growth. Kogan Page Publishers.

Chapter 3: The Art of Goal-Setting: SMART Criteria and Beyond

Doran, G. T. (1981). There's a S.M.A.R.T. way to write management's goals and objectives. Management Review, 70(11), 35-36.

Locke, E. A., & Latham, G. P. (2002). Building a practically useful theory of goal setting and task motivation: A 35-year odyssey. American Psychologist, 57(9), 705-717.

Rubin, R. S., Munz, D. C., & Bommer, W. H. (2005). Leading from within: The effects of emotion recognition and personality on transformational leadership behavior. Academy of Management Journal, 48(5), 845-858.

Dweck, C. S. (2006). Mindset: The new psychology of success. Random House Digital, Inc.

Schippers, M. C., & Homan, A. C. (2017). From ideal to real: A longitudinal study of the role of implicit leadership theories on leader-member exchanges and employee outcomes. Journal of Organizational Behavior, 38(6), 855-875.

Gollwitzer, P. M., & Oettingen, G. (2019). The power of planning and goal-setting. In Social psychology: Handbook of basic principles (pp. 375-394). Guilford Publications.

Chapter 4 The Science of Motivation: Intrinsic vs. Extrinsic Drivers

Deci, E. L., & Ryan, R. M. (2000). The "what" and "why" of goal pursuits: Human needs and the self-determination of behavior. Psychological Inquiry, 11(4), 227-268.

Pink, D. H. (2009). Drive: The surprising truth about what motivates us. Riverhead Books.

Ryan, R. M., & Deci, E. L. (2000). Intrinsic and extrinsic motivations: Classic definitions and new directions. Contemporary Educational Psychology, 25(1), 54-67.

Vansteenkiste, M., Simons, J., Lens, W., Sheldon, K. M., & Deci, E. L. (2004). Motivating learning, performance, and persistence: The synergistic effects of intrinsic goal contents and autonomy-supportive contexts. Journal of Personality and Social Psychology, 87(2), 246-260.

Additionally, the Google 20% Time program has been widely discussed in the media and popular books on company culture, such as "Creativity, Inc." by Ed Catmull.

Chapter 5: The Role of Values, Purpose, and Identity in Desired Outcomes

Deci, E. L., & Ryan, R. M. (2000). The "what" and "why" of goal pursuits: Human needs and the self-determination of behavior. Psychological Inquiry, 11(4), 227-268. doi: 10.1207/S15327965PLI1104_01

Emmons, R. A. (1986). Personal strivings: An approach to personality and subjective well-being. Journal of Personality and Social Psychology, 51(5), 1058-1068. doi: 10.1037/0022-3514.51.5.1058

Erikson, E. H. (1968). Identity: Youth and crisis. Norton.

Markus, H., & Wurf, E. (1987). The dynamic self-concept: A social psychological perspective. Annual Review of Psychology, 38(1), 299-337. doi: 10.1146/annurev.ps.38.020187.001503

Ryan, R. M., & Deci, E. L. (2000). Self-determination theory and the facilitation of intrinsic motivation, social development, and well-being. American Psychologist, 55(1), 68-78. doi: 10.1037/0003-066X.55.1.68

Chapter 6: The Power Trio: Visualization, Affirmation, and Meditation

Deci, E. L., & Ryan, R. M. (2000). The "what" and "why" of goal pursuits: Human needs and the self-determination of behavior. Psychological Inquiry, 11(4), 227-268. doi: 10.1207/S15327965PLI1104_01

Emmons, R. A. (1986). Personal strivings: An approach to personality and subjective well-being. Journal of Personality and Social Psychology, 51(5), 1058-1068. doi: 10.1037/0022-3514.51.5.1058

Erikson, E. H. (1968). Identity: Youth and crisis. Norton.

Markus, H., & Wurf, E. (1987). The dynamic self-concept: A social psychological perspective. Annual Review of Psychology, 38(1), 299-337. doi: 10.1146/annurev.ps.38.020187.001503

Ryan, R. M., & Deci, E. L. (2000). Self-determination theory and the facilitation of intrinsic motivation, social development, and well-being. American Psychologist, 55(1), 68-78. doi: 10.1037/0003-066X.55.1.68

Chapter 7: The Cognitive Skills, Abilities, and Intuitive Thinking that Drive Success

Dweck, C. S. (2008). Mindset: The new psychology of success. Random House Digital, Inc.

Edmondson, A. (2019). The fearless organization: Creating psychological safety in the workplace for learning, innovation, and growth. John Wiley & Sons.

Johnson, S. (2013). The Innovator's Dilemma: When New Technologies Cause Great Firms to Fail. Harvard Business Review Press.

Kahneman, D. (2011). Thinking, fast and slow. Macmillan.

Liker, J. K. (2014). The Toyota way to continuous improvement: linking strategy and operational excellence to achieve superior performance. McGraw-Hill.

Martin, R. (2009). The design of business: Why design thinking is the next competitive advantage. Harvard Business Press.

Senge, P. M. (2006). The fifth discipline: The art and practice of the learning organization. Crown Business.

Sutherland, J. (2014). Scrum: The art of doing twice the work in half the time. Random House.Syed, M. (2016). Black box thinking: Marginal gains and the secrets of high performance. John Murray.

Kahneman, D. (2011). Thinking, fast and slow. Macmillan.

Gladwell, M. (2005). Blink: The power of thinking without thinking. Little, Brown.

Gigerenzer, G. (2007). Gut feelings: The intelligence of the unconscious. Penguin.

Pink, D. H. (2005). A whole new mind: Why right-brainers will rule the future. Penguin.

Dijksterhuis, A. (2014). The intuitive psychologist and his shortcomings: Distortions in the attribution process. Psychology Press.

Simon, H. A. (1983). Reasoning and decision-making in psychology and economics. The American Economic Review, 73(2), 129-132.

Chapter 8: Positive Thinking: Unlocking Your Path to Success and Happiness

Boehm, J. K., & Kubzansky, L. D. (2012). The heart's content: The association between positive psychological well-being and cardiovascular health. Psychological Bulletin, 138(4), 655-691.

Chida, Y., & Steptoe, A. (2008). Positive psychological well-being and mortality: A quantitative review of prospective observational studies. Psychosomatic Medicine, 70(7), 741-756

Lyubomirsky, S., King, L., & Diener, E. (2005). The benefits of frequent positive affect: Does happiness lead to success? Psychological Bulletin, 131(6), 803-855.

Spreitzer, G. M., & Sonenshein, S. (2004). Toward the construct definition of positive deviance. American Behavioral Scientist, 47(6), 828-847.

Chapter 9: Mapping Your Terrain: PESTLE Analysis and Environmental Scanning

Grant, R. M. (2016). Contemporary strategy analysis: Text and cases edition. John Wiley & Sons.

Johnson, G., Scholes, K., & Whittington, R. (2019). Exploring strategy: Text and cases. Pearson Education Limited.

Lynch, R. (2015). Strategic management. Pearson Education Limited.

Makos, J. (2017). Environmental scanning as a key determinant of organizational success. Journal of Business and Economics Research, 15(4), 87-96.

Nieuwenhuizen, C. (2018). Business management: A contemporary approach. Juta and Company Ltd.

Tesla. (2022). Tesla, Inc. Retrieved from https://www.tesla.com/

Chapter 10: Developing Your Strategy: SWOT Matrix
Thompson, A. A., Peteraf, M. A., Gamble, J. E., & Strickland III, A. J. (2020). Crafting and executing strategy: The quest for competitive advantage: Concepts and cases. McGraw-Hill Education.

Grant, R. M. (2016). Contemporary strategy analysis: Text and cases edition. John Wiley & Sons.

Wheelen, T. L., & Hunger, J. D. (2017). Strategic management and business policy: Globalization, innovation and sustainability. Pearson.

Hill, C. W., & Jones, G. R. (2017). Strategic management: An integrated approach. Cengage Learning.

Porter, M. E. (2008). The five competitive forces that shape strategy. Harvard Business Review, 86(1), 78-93.

Johnson, G., Whittington, R., Scholes, K., Angwin, D., & Regner, P. (2017). Exploring strategy: Text and cases. Pearson.

Armstrong, M. (2019). Armstrong's handbook of strategic human resource management. Kogan Page Publishers.

Chapter 11: Developing Your Strategy: Porter's Five Forces

Porter, M.E. (1979). "How competitive forces shape strategy." Harvard Business Review, March-April 1979, pp. 137-145.

Porter, M.E. (2008). "The five competitive forces that shape strategy." Harvard Business Review, January 2008, pp. 78-93.

Grant, R.M. (2016). Contemporary Strategy Analysis: Text and Cases Edition (9th ed.). Wiley-Blackwell.

Hill, C.W.L., & Jones, G.R. (2017). Strategic Management: An Integrated Approach (12th ed.). Cengage Learning.

Johnson, G., Whittington, R., Scholes, K., Angwin, D., & Regner, P. (2017). Exploring Strategy: Text and Cases (11th ed.). Pearson Education Limited.

Chapter 12: Creating Your Action Plan: To-Do Lists, and Milestones
"Gantt Chart." Investopedia, Investopedia, 25 Aug. 2021, www.investopedia.com/terms/g/ganttchart.asp.

Bowerman, Chris. "7 Online Tools That Will Help You Create Beautiful Gantt Charts." The Daily Egg, Crazy Egg, Inc., 19 Mar. 2020, www.crazyegg.com/blog/gantt-chart-tools.

"To-Do List." Wikipedia, Wikimedia Foundation, 31 Mar. 2023, en.wikipedia.org/wiki/To-do_list.

Allen, David. Getting Things Done: The Art of Stress-Free Productivity. Penguin Books, 2015.

"Milestones." Mind Tools, Mind Tools, Ltd., 2021, www.mindtools.com/pages/article/newPPM_03.htm.

Geron, Tomio. "Airbnb Co-Founder Shares His Secret for Scaling a Startup: The Business Plan." Forbes, Forbes Magazine, 4 Sept. 2012, www.forbes.com/sites/tomiogeron/2012/09/04/airbnb-co-founder-shares-his-secret-for-scaling-a-startup-the-business-plan/?sh=680f9c3866cd.

"Airbnb." Wikipedia, Wikimedia Foundation, 29 Mar. 2023, en.wikipedia.org/wiki/Airbnb.

Chapter 13: Building Your Support Network: Mentors, Allies, and Accountability Partners

"Lean In: Women, Work, and the Will to Lead" by Sheryl Sandberg

Lean In website. "What Are Circles?" Accessed at: https://leanin.org/sheryl-sandbergs-circle#!

"The Power of Mentors, Advocates and Allies in Career Advancement" by Jo Miller

"Accountability Partners: How to Stay on Track and Reach Your Goals" by Paige Brettingen

"The Art of Mentoring: Lead, Follow, and Get Out of the Way" by Darrell W. Gunter and J. Kim Wright

"Networking for People Who Hate Networking: A Field Guide for Introverts, the Overwhelmed, and the Under connected" by Devora Zack

Chapter 14: Managing Your Resources: Time, Money, and Energy

Covey, S. R. (1994). The 7 habits of highly effective people: Powerful lessons in personal change. Free Press.

Tracy, B. (2013). Time management. Amacom.

Ramsey, D. (2017). The total money makeover: A proven plan for financial fitness. Thomas Nelson.

Orman, S. (2006). Women & money: Owning the power to control your destiny. Spiegel & Grau.

Loehr, J., & Schwartz, T. (2003). The power of full engagement: Managing energy, not time, is the key to high performance and personal renewal. Free Press.

Hymowitz, C., & Koczwara, A. (2018). Bad blood: Secrets and lies in a Silicon Valley startup. John Murray.

Carreyrou, J. (2018). Bad blood: Secrets and lies in a Silicon Valley startup. Knopf Doubleday Publishing Group.

Chapter 15: Cultivating Your Skills and Knowledge: Learning Plans and Self-Development
Covey, S. R. (2004). The 7 habits of highly effective people: Powerful lessons in personal change. Simon and Schuster.

Dweck, C. S. (2006). Mindset: The new psychology of success. Random House.
Pink, D. H. (2011). Drive: The surprising truth about what motivates us. Riverhead Books.

Sinek, S. (2011). Start with why: How great leaders inspire everyone to take action. Penguin.

Sprenger, M. (2003). Becoming a lifelong learner: Strategies for identifying and achieving your goals. John Wiley & Sons.

Stillman, Jessica. (September 2020) "Brown, Brene: You Can't Change Your Life Without Loving Yourself First:. Inc. Accessed at: https://www.inc.com/jessica-stillman/brene-brown-success-self-love.html

Thompson, L. (2020). The Power of Learning: Cultivating a Lifelong Love of Learning. Routledge.

Zimmerman, B. J. (2008). Investigating self-regulation and motivation: Historical background, methodological developments, and future prospects. American Educational Research Journal, 45(1), 166-183.

Zimmerman, B. J., & Schunk, D. H. (2011). Handbook of self-regulation of learning and performance. Routledge.

Chapter 16: Assessing Your Progress: Key Performance Indicators and Metrics

Key Performance Indicators: Developing, Implementing, and Using Winning KPIs by David Parmenter (2010)

Key Performance Indicators (KPI): Developing, Implementing, and Using Winning KPIs by Bernard Marr (2016)

Performance Management: Integrating Strategy Execution, Methodologies, Risk, and Analytics by Gary Cokins (2019)

Measuring What Matters: How Google, Bono, and the Gates Foundation Rock the World with OKRs by John Doerr (2018)

The Lean Startup: How Today's Entrepreneurs Use Continuous Innovation to Create Radically Successful Businesses by Eric Ries (2011)

Setting Goals, by Simone Biles, MasterClass.com
https://www.masterclass.com/classes/simone-biles-teaches-gymnastics-fundamentals/chapters/setting-goals

Chapter 17: Overcoming Obstacles: Procrastination, Perfectionism, and Self-Sabotage

Steel, P. (2007). The nature of procrastination: A meta-analytic and theoretical review of quintessential self-regulatory failure. Psychological bulletin, 133(1), 65-94.

Flett, G. L., Hewitt, P. L., Blankstein, K. R., & Mosher, S. W. (1995). Perfectionism, negative social feedback, and depression. Journal of social and clinical psychology, 14(4), 360-371.

Sirois, F. M., Melia-Gordon, M. L., & Pychyl, T. A. (2018). "I'll look after my health later": A replication and extension of the procrastination-health model with community-dwelling adults. Personality and Individual Differences, 124, 179-183.

Klingsieck, K. B. (2013). Procrastination: When good things don't come to those who wait. European psychologist, 18(1), 24-34.

Hewitt, P. L., & Flett, G. L. (1991). Perfectionism in the self and social contexts: Conceptualization, assessment, and association with psychopathology. Journal of personality and social psychology, 60(3), 456-470.

Chapter 18: Facing Your Fears: Failure, Rejection, and Criticism

Brown, B. (2012). Daring greatly: How the courage to be vulnerable transforms the way we live, love, parent, and lead. Gotham Books.

Duckworth, A. L. (2016). Grit: The power of passion and perseverance. Scribner.

Newman, R. (2018). You can't wear out your voice: 10 tips for confidence, resilience and leadership for women who want to speak up. Tell Me Press.

Sincero, J. (2013). You are a badass: How to stop doubting your greatness and start living an awesome life. Running Press.

Stone, D., & Heen, S. (2014). Thanks for the feedback: The science and art of receiving feedback well. Penguin.

Dweck, C. S. (2007). Mindset: The new psychology of success. Random House.

Grant, A. M. (2013). Give and take: A revolutionary approach to success. Penguin Books.

Kets de Vries, M. F. R. (2014). Reflections on leadership and career development: On the couch with Manfred Kets de Vries. Palgrave Macmillan.

Chapter 19: Learning from Feedback: Feedback Loops, Surveys, and Reviews

Brown, B. (2012). Daring greatly: How the courage to be vulnerable transforms the way we live, love, parent, and lead. Gotham Books.

Duckworth, A. L. (2016). Grit: The power of passion and perseverance. Scribner.

Newman, R. (2018). You can't wear out your voice: 10 tips for confidence, resilience and leadership for women who want to speak up. Tell Me Press.

Sincero, J. (2013). You are a badass: How to stop doubting your greatness and start living an awesome life. Running Press.

Stone, D., & Heen, S. (2014). Thanks for the feedback: The science and art of receiving feedback well. Penguin.

Dweck, C. S. (2007). Mindset: The new psychology of success. Random House.

Grant, A. M. (2013). Give and take: A revolutionary approach to success. Penguin Books.

Kets de Vries, M. F. R. (2014). Reflections on leadership and career development: On the couch with Manfred Kets de Vries. Palgrave Macmillan.

Chapter 20: Staying on Track: Habit Formation, Routines, and Rituals

Brown, B. (2012). Daring greatly: How the courage to be vulnerable transforms the way we live, love, parent, and lead. Gotham Books.

Duckworth, A. L. (2016). Grit: The power of passion and perseverance. Scribner.
Newman, R. (2018). You can't wear out your voice: 10 tips for confidence, resilience and leadership for women who want to speak up. Tell Me Press.

Sincero, J. (2013). You are a badass: How to stop doubting your greatness and start living an awesome life. Running Press.

Stone, D., & Heen, S. (2014). Thanks for the feedback: The science and art of receiving feedback well. Penguin.

Dweck, C. S. (2007). Mindset: The new psychology of success. Random House.
Grant, A. M. (2013). Give and take: A revolutionary approach to success. Penguin Books.

Kets de Vries, M. F. R. (2014). Reflections on leadership and career development: On the couch with Manfred Kets de Vries. Palgrave Macmillan.

Chapter 21: Sustaining Your Momentum: Continuous Improvement and Growth Mindset

Dweck, C. S. (2016). Mindset: The new psychology of success. Random House.

Imai, M. (1986). Kaizen: The key to Japan's competitive success. Random House.

Duckworth, A. L., Peterson, C., Matthews, M. D., & Kelly, D. R. (2007). Grit: Perseverance and passion for long-term goals. Journal of personality and social psychology, 92(6), 1087–1101.

Shen, W., & Cho, Y. J. (2019). Continuous improvement: A review and research agenda. International Journal of Production Research, 57(3), 787-813.

Johnson, D. (2019). The Rock: Through the Lens: His Life, His Movies, His World. Houghton Mifflin Harcourt.
Johnson, D. (2017). The Rock's Ultimate Workout. Muscle and Fitness. Retrieved from https://www.muscleandfitness.com/workouts/workout-routines/rock-s-ultimate-workout/

Johnson, D. (2020). The Rock on the Power of Positivity. Oprah Magazine. Retrieved from https://www.oprahmag.com/entertainment/tv-movies/a33060434/the-rock-interview/

Serrat, O. (2017). Understanding and Leading Organizational Change Management. In Knowledge Solutions (pp. 265-277). Springer.

Chapter 22: Celebrating Your Achievements: Milestone Parties, Gratitude Journals, and Rewards

"The Psychology of Celebrating Your Wins" by Sarah Green Carmichael (Harvard Business Review)

"Why Celebrating Small Wins is Essential to Your Long-Term Success" by Belle Beth Cooper (Buffer blog)

"Why Gratitude is Good" by Robert A. Emmons and Anjali Mishra (Greater Good Magazine)https://www.mindtools.com/pages/article/newHTE_92.htm

Positive Psychology: https://positivepsychology.com/celebrate-success-achieve-more/

Forbes: https://www.forbes.com/sites/ashleystahl/2018/08/01/how-to-celebrate-your-success-when-youre-an-entrepreneur/?sh=748d9e835e2dMacmillan.

Chapter 23: Making Your Desired Outcome a Legacy: Giving Back, Paying Forward, and Contributing to Society

Giving back: The benefits of giving back to society, by Maryville University, https://online.maryville.edu/blog/benefits-of-giving-back-to-society/

Paying it forward: The power of paying it forward, by Forbes, https://www.forbes.com/sites/ashleystahl/2021/02/15/the-power-of-paying-it-forward/?sh=2ee29dd84e2d

Contributing to society: Ways to contribute to society, by University of Arizona, https://online.arizona.edu/blog/ways-contribute-society

Bill Gates case study: Bill and Melinda Gates Foundation, by Bill and Melinda Gates Foundation, https://www.gatesfoundation.org/

Malala Yousafzai case study: Malala Fund, by Malala Fund, https://www.malala.org/

About the Author

Wes Berry is a Keynote Speaker and Workshop Facilitator with the professional skills and real-life experience to deliver on any stage. He works with Fortune 500 companies like Johnson & Johnson to smaller businesses and associations of all sizes that are seeking a breakthrough experience. Wes changes lives and transforms organizations by delivering a Paradigm Shift. He has written sixteen business and success books and is a *Wall Street Journal* best-selling author and TEDx speaker. As an entrepreneur, he built a $750 million international company that operated in 130 countries.

His business knowledge and communications skills have made him an expert media contributor on many topics, from commercial drone applications to the downsizing of Sears, resulting in appearances with various media outlets. His many media appearances include NPR, *The Wall Street Journal*, *The London Times*, *Entrepreneur* and *Time* magazines, Fox News, Neil Cavuto, Geraldo Rivera, and John Stossel, to name just a few.

Visit his website at WesBerryGroup.com to learn more.

www.ingramcontent.com/pod-product-compliance
Lightning Source LLC
LaVergne TN
LVHW020431070526
838199LV00025B/596/J